the
Political
Spectrum

OPPOSING VIEWPOINTS

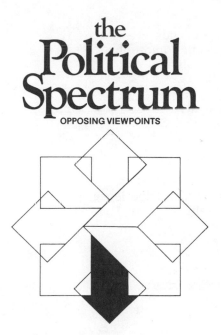

Other Books of Related Interest in the Opposing Viewpoints Series:

American Foreign Policy
The American Military
American Values
Economics in America
The Welfare State

Additional Books in the Opposing Viewpoints Series:

Abortion
America's Prisons
The Arms Race
Censorship
Central America
Chemical Dependency
Constucting a Life Philosophy
Crime & Criminals
Criminal Justice
Death & Dying
The Death Penalty
The Environmental Crisis
Male/Female Roles
The Middle East
Nuclear War
Problems of Africa
Religion and Human Experience
Science and Religion
Sexual Values
Social Justice
Terrorism
The Vietnam War
War and Human Nature

the
Political
Spectrum

OPPOSING VIEWPOINTS

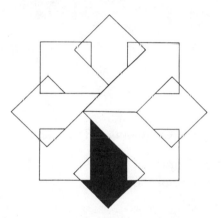

David L. Bender/Bruno Leone

OPPOSING VIEWPOINTS SERIES ®

Greenhaven Press   577 Shoreview Park Road   St. Paul, Minnesota 55126

Library of Congress Cataloging-in-Publication Data

The Political spectrum.

  (Opposing viewpoints series)
  Bibliography: p.
  Includes index.
  1. Political science—United States. 2. Right and left (Political science) I. Bender, David L., 1936-   . II. Leone, Bruno, 1939-   . III. Series.
JA84.U5P612 1986   320.5'0973   86-19415
ISBN 0-89908-392-7
ISBN 0-89908-367-6 (pbk.)

"Congress shall make no law...
abridging the freedom of speech,
or of the press."

First Amendment to the US Constitution

The basic foundation of our democracy is the first amendment guarantee of freedom of expression. The *Opposing Viewpoints Series* is dedicated to the concept of this basic freedom and the idea that it is more important to practice it than to enshrine it.

Contents

Why Consider Opposing Viewpoints?

"It is better to debate a question without settling it than to settle a question without debating it."

Joseph Joubert (1754-1824)

The Importance of Examining Opposing Viewpoints

The purpose of the Opposing Viewpoints Series, and this book in particular, is to present balanced, and often difficult to find, opposing points of view on complex and sensitive issues.

Probably the best way to become informed is to analyze the positions of those who are regarded as experts and well studied on issues. It is important to consider every variety of opinion in an attempt to determine the truth. Opinions from the mainstream of society should be examined. But also important are opinions that are considered radical, reactionary, or minority as well as those stigmatized by some other uncomplimentary label. An important lesson of history is the eventual acceptance of many unpopular and even despised opinions. The ideas of Socrates, Jesus, and Galileo are good examples of this.

Readers will approach this book with their own opinions on the issues debated within it. However, to have a good grasp of one's own viewpoint, it is necessary to understand the arguments of those with whom one disagrees. It can be said that those who do not completely understand their adversary's point of view do not fully understand their own.

A persuasive case for considering opposing viewpoints has been presented by John Stuart Mill in his work *On Liberty*. When examining controversial issues it may be helpful to reflect on this suggestion:

> The only way in which a human being can make some approach to knowing the whole of a subject, is by hearing what can be said about it by persons of every variety of opinion, and studying all modes in which it can be looked at by every character of mind. No wise man ever acquired his wisdom in any mode but this.

Analyzing Sources of Information

The Opposing Viewpoints Series includes diverse materials taken from magazines, journals, books, and newspapers, as well as statements and position papers from a wide range of individuals, organizations and governments. This broad spectrum of sources helps to develop patterns of thinking which are open to the consideration of a variety of opinions.

Pitfalls to Avoid

A pitfall to avoid in considering opposing points of view is that of regarding one's own opinion as being common sense and the most rational stance and the point of view of others as being only opinion and naturally wrong. It may be that another's opinion is correct and one's own is in error.

Another pitfall to avoid is that of closing one's mind to the opinions of those with whom one disagrees. The best way to approach a dialogue is to make one's primary purpose that of understanding the mind and arguments of the other person and not that of enlightening him or her with one's own solutions. More can be learned by listening than speaking.

It is my hope that after reading this book the reader will have a deeper understanding of the issues debated and will appreciate the complexity of even seemingly simple issues on which good and honest people disagree. This awareness is particularly important in a democratic society such as ours where people enter into public debate to determine the common good. Those with whom one disagrees should not necessarily be regarded as enemies, but perhaps simply as people who suggest different paths to a common goal.

Developing Basic Reading and Thinking Skills

In this book, carefully edited opposing viewpoints are purposely placed back to back to create a running debate; each viewpoint is preceded by a short quotation that best expresses the author's main argument. This format instantly plunges the reader into the midst of a controversial issue and greatly aids that reader in mastering the basic skill of recognizing an author's point of view.

A number of basic skills for critical thinking are practiced in the activities that appear throughout the books in the series. Some of the skills are:

Evaluating Sources of Information The ability to choose from among alternative sources the most reliable and accurate source in relation to a given subject.

Separating Fact from Opinion The ability to make the basic distinction between factual statements (those that can be demonstrated or verified empirically) and statements of opinion (those that are beliefs or attitudes that cannot be proved).

Identifying Stereotypes The ability to identify oversimplified, exaggerated descriptions (favorable or unfavorable) about people and insulting statements about racial, religious or national groups, based upon misinformation or lack of information.

Recognizing Ethnocentrism The ability to recognize attitudes or opinions that express the view that one's own race, culture, or group is inherently superior, or those attitudes that judge another culture or group in terms of one's own.

It is important to consider opposing viewpoints and equally important to be able to critically analyze those viewpoints. The activities in this book are designed to help the reader master these thinking skills. Statements are taken from the book's viewpoints and the reader is asked to analyze them. This technique aids the reader in developing skills that not only can be applied to the viewpoints in this book, but also to situations where opinionated spokespersons comment on controversial issues. Although the activities are helpful to the solitary reader, they are most useful when the reader can benefit from the interaction of group discussion.

Using this book and others in the series should help readers develop basic reading and thinking skills. These skills should improve the reader's ability to understand what they read. Readers should be better able to separate fact from opinion, substance from rhetoric and become better consumers of information in our media-centered culture.

This volume of the Opposing Viewpoints Series does not advocate a particular point of view. Quite the contrary! The very nature of the book leaves it to the reader to formulate the opinions he or she finds most suitable. My purpose as publisher is to see that this is made possible by offering a wide range of viewpoints which are fairly presented.

David L. Bender
Publisher

Introduction

"In a representative form of government there are usually two general schools of political belief—liberal and conservative."

Franklin Delano Roosevelt, 1938

The terms liberal and conservative, always difficult to define, are even more of a mystery in contemporary America. Franklin Roosevelt, a saint of American liberalism and the architect of its New Deal programs, is now also claimed by conservatives. The Reagan presidency, viewed by many as the most conservative administration in the post World War Two era, also claims Roosevelt as a patron saint. What is the average American to think? Who are today's liberals and conservatives, and what principles and issues distinguish them? The matter is further complicated with the recent introduction of two new terms, *neoliberal* and *neoconservative*. Who are they?

The purpose of this book is to identify the basic differences that separate liberals and conservatives and to outline the contemporary political spectrum in American life. The first chapter presents different views of the political spectrum. It suggests outlines to use in comparing liberalism and conservatism. The reader will discover that disagreement even exists over how to graphically depict the political spectrum. The chapter presents current thinking on how to diagram the spectrum but it is left to the reader to choose the graphic representation that he or she finds most helpful.

Chapter Two presents the views of several political philosophers and statesmen from the past. The ideas of these thinkers represent some of the philosophical wellsprings from which modern-day liberalism and conservatism have grown. A knowledge of the works of these and other earlier theorists is important in understanding the evolutionary changes the political spectrum has experienced.

The last two chapters present arguments by prominent liberals and conservatives, taken from the past three decades of American life. In these chapters, supporters and opponents of both principles debate the philosophical and practical value of these *isms*. Each chapter is concluded with a viewpoint by the main spokesperson of each *isms'* newest movement: *Neoliberalism* and *neoconservatism*

13

are terms one sees frequently these days on the political landscape. An understanding of their meanings is necessary to complete one's understanding of the political spectrum.

The most elusive part of the political spectrum, extremism, is not included in this book for two reasons. First, space would not permit an adequate coverage of the subject. More importantly, *Extremism: Opposing Viewpoints* is the title of a future volume that will be added to the Opposing Viewpoints Series. It will serve as a companion to this volume.

What Is America's Political Spectrum?

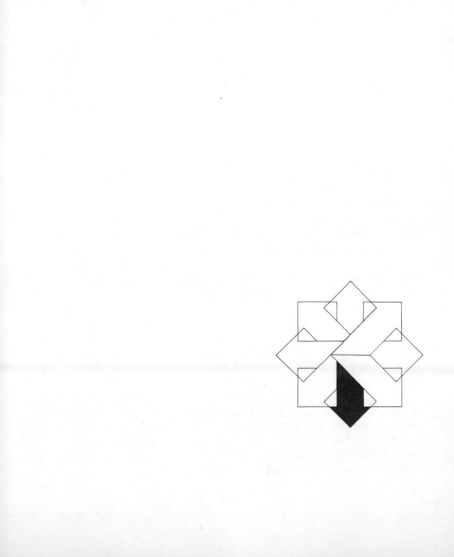

Chapter Preface

What do the terms liberal and conservative signify, and are they helpful or confusing labels in contemporary America? Does the traditional bipolar, straight-line continuum present an accurate description of the current situation, or is a new symbolic representation necessary? These are the main issues debated in this chapter.

For years teachers, columnists, and others have confidently used words such as liberal, conservative, and right- or left-winger to describe political reality in America. Recently the political lexicon has been expanded. New terms, or old terms with new meanings, such as libertarian, populist, neoconservative, and neoliberal, sometimes describing the same group or phenomenon, have been added. For example, the word *populist* currently identifies an individual different than his 19th century namesake. Change, a basic issue that has always divided liberals and conservatives, has altered appraisals of the political spectrum.

The viewpoints in this chapter present different perspectives of the current political spectrum. They also describe the contemporary meaning of the terms mentioned above. By studying and comparing these viewpoints, the reader should acquire an overview of the spectrum and an understanding of basic political terms that are vital to contemporary American life.

"The traditional bipolar, straight-line continuum . . . is a model that many are familiar with and it provides an easily understood overview of the different perspectives of liberals and conservatives."

The Traditional Spectrum Is Still Useful

David L. Bender

David Bender is an editor of this volume and the publisher and originator of the "Opposing Viewpoints Series." A former high school social problems teacher, he has edited numerous titles in the series, most recently *Constructing a Life Philosophy: Opposing Viewpoints* (1985). In the following viewpoint, he presents a case for the usefulness of the bipolar, or two-ended, straight-line continuum political spectrum. He also catalogs the distinguishing marks of liberals and conservatives, claiming their greatest difference is their conflicting appraisals of human nature.

As you read, consider the following questions:

1. In the author's opinion, why is the bipolar, straight-line continuum view of the political spectrum a useful concept?
2. What two basic distinctions does he make between liberals and conservatives?
3. What does he mean when he claims that at the root of the liberal/conservative debate is a basic disagreement about human nature?

This viewpoint was written for this book. An earlier version of it appeared in David L. Bender, *Liberals and Conservatives: A Debate on the Welfare State*. Minneapolis: Greenhaven Press, 1973.

The terms liberal, conservative, extremist, and more recently, neoliberal and neoconservative, appear frequently in print and in common usage. It is difficult to pick up the editorial pages of any newspaper without reading about the in-fighting of liberals and conservatives in congress or elsewhere on the political landscape. One hears frequently of various extremist groups, religious, political or other, at work somewhere in American society. In spite of their frequent appearance, it is doubtful that the average individual has more than a vague understanding of these terms and the differences they signify. Because these labels are so frequently used, it is important that the interested observer of the American scene be familiar with their meaning.

The Traditional View of the Spectrum Is Most Helpful

The political spectrum has been visualized in a number of ways, including a circle, a diamond, and even the half-moon shaped guide on an automobile's automatic transmission shifter by a creative Pennsylvania high school teacher.[1] I prefer the traditional bipolar, straight-line continuum. It is a model that many are familiar with and it provides an easily understood overview of the different perspectives of liberals and conservatives. For readers concerned about the validity of this description of liberals and conservatives in the late 1980s, I invite them to read the Conover and Feldman study for an analysis of its current usefulness.[2] As any good conservative would reason, if it works why fix it.

Because ideological differences are slight in America, in comparison to most other societies, a graphic visualization can greatly aid the reader's understanding of the sometimes subtle differences that separate liberals and conservatives. Consensus, leavened with compromise, not impassioned zeal for an ideological cause, has always been America's driving force. Ironically, in spite of our melting pot heritage, we Americans are more alike than different. Yet, we do not all see issues through the same lenses. There are real differences between liberals and conservatives.

This viewpoint will outline the differences between liberals, conservatives, neoliberals, and neoconservatives. Before continuing the reader should be cautioned. The following descriptions are necessarily brief and simplified. Although a danger of brevity can be distortion, these descriptions are presented in the belief that they will provide a helpful overview of the basic orientations of liberals and conservatives and the differences that distinguish them. Those who wish to become familiar with subtle distinctions and basic disagreements within liberal or conservative camps will have to pursue the issues independently. The annotated bibliography at the end of this book would be a good place to begin.

One may distinguish between American liberals and conservatives in two ways, their readiness to change and their philosophical differences. Let us first consider their readiness to accept or bring about change.

Readiness to Change

If one were to construct a continuum showing reaction to change, the following stopping points would be noted.

The Political Spectrum

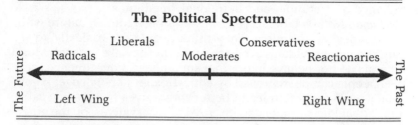

Radicals and liberals are called left-wingers or leftists and generally welcome change. Conservatives and reactionaries are called right-wingers or rightists and are reluctant to accept change. Each position on the continuum can be defined as follows.

The Radical	Favors a radical or basic change— quite impatient and would quickly support a revolution to bring about the desired change.
The Liberal	Ready to move forward and accept change but would be considered a reformer rather than a revolutionary.
The Conservative	Quite content with things the way they are.
The Reactionary	Desires change also, but wants to retreat into the past and restore the order of times remembered.

A former advisor of Franklin D. Roosevelt's, Rexford Tugwell, skillfully used the example of a community's need for a new train station to illustrate the difference between liberals and radicals. He claimed "liberals would like to rebuild the station while the trains are running; radicals prefer to blow up the station and forego service until the new structure is built."[3] One might add that conservatives would prefer to keep the old station, being satisfied with it, while reactionaries would abandon the station entirely since they do not approve of trains in the first place.[4]

Whatever the differences between the left-wing and the right-wing in accepting change, all four viewpoints can be helpful to society. The radical points out the future's possibilities while the liberal helps to see them realized through the practice of compromise. The conservative cautions us to preserve existing accomplishments and the reactionary reminds us of our heritage and the glory of times past.

Philosophical Differences

More important than their readiness to change are the philosophical differences that separate liberals and conservatives. The greatest areas of disagreement concern human nature, reliance on tradition, and individual freedom.

Human Nature: Liberals generally approach human nature with a great deal of optimism. They think people are basically good, and though individuals are born ignorant they are not evil. Most liberals do not believe in original sin and as a consequence they feel people can be improved by education and knowledge. If you give people opportunities to better themselves they will usually take advantage of them and improve. Conservatives, on the other hand, have a more pessimistic opinion of human nature. Because they believe people have been tainted by original sin, or are otherwise flawed, they expect less of people. They are more reluctant to provide welfare programs such as aid to dependent children or unemployment compensation, because they do not think it will be used properly, and in fact think it will cause additional problems as the weaker tendencies of human nature will be reinforced. Liberals welcome reforms because they feel that human history is one of continual progress as people inform and improve themselves.

Liberals also favor rapid movement toward constitutional or democratic forms of government because of their great confidence in the ability of the enlightened citizen to make wise and prudent choices at the ballot box. Conservatives are distrustful of the average citizen's ability to direct a government, even only indirectly as in a representative democracy such as the United States.[5]

Tradition and Reform: The second philosophical difference between liberals and conservatives, reliance on tradition, is somewhat related to their readiness to change. One of the fundamental values of conservatism is a confidence in the accumulated wisdom and traditions of the past. Conservatives do not favor quick change for they fear it may bring negative results. They point out that the positive accomplishments of humanity have been the result of gradual change and slow growth. They do not, like liberals, advocate utopian forms of government, for they are skeptical of unproven theories and the possibility of people improving their condition greatly in a short period of time. Conservatives prefer the status quo, which they consider the end result of centuries of experience and knowledge. Conservatives historically have felt little need to articulate their philosophy, for it represents the system that presently exists. Liberals, on the other hand, impatient for improvement, are frequently presenting arguments and programs

20

to change the current system.

Russell Kirk, perhaps America's preeminent conservative spokesman, defines tradition as a set of "received opinions, convictions religious and moral and political and aesthetic passed down from generation to generation, so that they are accepted by most men as a matter of course."[6] Conservatives are satisfied to live with tradition. Liberals continually question established opinions and convictions, whether they be religious, moral, political or social.

Authority and Individual Freedom: Closely allied to the difference of opinion on the importance of tradition is the disagreement over authority versus individual freedom. Because liberals expect people to act correctly when they are informed they allow them a great amount of liberty in their actions. Conservatives however, not having such an optimistic opinion of people, feel they must often be controlled for their own best interests.

Wolf or Lamb?

The conservative errs in regarding man as though he were a wolf; the liberal errs in regarding man as though he were a lamb; neither will concede that man is both in nearly equal portion.

Sydney Harris, Field Enterprises, April 1980.

A partial understanding of the disagreement on the topic of individual freedom as opposed to institutionalized authority can be gained by simply defining the terms liberal and conservative. Liberal is derived from the early nineteenth-century Spanish political party, the *Liberales*, a party that advocated a constitutional form of government that would grant more freedom to individuals than the established authoritarian government it was opposing. The world "liberal" has since come to signify any idea, individual, movement, or party that favors granting more individual liberty than the traditional authoritarian forms of government normally permit. The term "conservative" means literally to conserve, namely the traditions, customs and governments that have evolved through many generations of human experience.

Again, because of liberals' optimistic outlook, they believe that people will use wisely liberties given them. Conservatives, however, believe that people must frequently be restrained and guided by those in society who are more educated and better equipped to govern. Edmund Burke, who is often referred to as the father of modern conservatism, expressed the conservative's aversion to giving too much freedom to the individual.

The extreme of liberty . . . obtains nowhere, nor ought to obtain

21

anywhere; because extremes, as we all know, in every point which relates either to our duties or satisfactions in life, are destructive both to virtue and enjoyment. Liberty, too, must be limited in order to be possessed.[7]

It should be obvious to the reader that the philosophical differences that separate liberals and conservatives spring from their basic disagreement on human nature and its perfectibility. One could cite other philosophical issues such as equality, rationalism versus tradition, intellectual freedom and censorship, the role and scope of government, and the nature of religion, topics that all cause a direct confrontation between liberals and conservatives. But at the root of all these disagreements is the central question concerning human nature, the basic goodness and perfectability of people and their tendencies toward weakness, evil, and selfishness.

The Neo Movements

During the late 1970s and into the 1980s two new words have been introduced into the political spectrum lexicon, neoconservative and neoliberal. Each of these terms represents shifts within liberal and conservative camps and emphasizes tactics and stances on issues more than ideological restructuring. The terms paleoconservative and paleoliberal have also been coined to distinguish neos from their more traditional brethren.

The neoconservative movement is the most visible of the two and seems to be more substantive in terms of an identifiable program and self-proclaimed disciples. Its principal founder is Irving Kristol who presents the case for neoconservatism in chapter four of this book. Other prominent neoconservatives are Norman Podhoretz, the editor of *Commentary*, Charles Murray, Michael Novak, and Midge Decter.

Neoliberalism's founder, Charles Peters, also founded its movement's most prominent publication, *The Washington Monthly*. He presents the case for neoliberalism in chapter three. Others who have advanced neoliberal ideas are James Fallows, Washington editor of *The Atlantic*, and senators Gary Hart and Bill Bradley.

Both neoconservatives and neoliberals stress the importance of economic growth. They are disillusioned about the growth and bureaucratization of government over the past fifty years. They differ in the respect that neoliberals favor central economic planning and government involvement in providing for the poor, creating jobs, guaranteeing health care, retraining displaced workers, protecting consumers, protecting the environment, and additional programs. Neoconservatives, on the other hand, favor less government, decentralization, and letting the marketplace function with little government interference. They also advocate traditional family values, an aggressive, nationalistic foreign policy, and a strengthened defense department.

In terms of change, society is constantly moving to the left on the spectrum as suggested social reforms become adopted programs. At the same time, unless individuals and organizations adapt, there is a tendency for them to become more conservative as they remain stationary while society moves to the left.

Walk or Run

I believe that liberals tend to design houses, conservatives to build them. The liberal mind, by and large, moves more quickly than the conservative's to original thought.

Those of us on the right tend to stand by tradition, precedent, and the old ways of doing things; those on the left are more impatient to get on with the job.

James J. Kilpatrick, *Washington Star,* May 1973.

An example of society's leftward movement is the advocacy of social security payments for elderly Americans. Those who advocated such payments in 1900 probably would have been called radicals by their contemporaries for asking for such a significant change in America's social and economic structures. If these individuals had advocated the same program in 1935, when the Roosevelt administration pushed through the Social Security Act making it a reality, they would have been called liberals on the issue. If they were to maintain the same position on the issue in the 1950s, long after the social security program was adopted and accepted by the public, they would have been called conservatives for supporting the status quo. By the 1980s, the original social security program had been expanded by additional benefits and larger pension payments. If our hypothetical individuals were to advocate a return to the same original program they supported in 1900 and 1935 they would be called reactionaries for wanting to return to the past.

There is a possibility this same phenomenon may also be observed in the Democratic party. Will the party that has been associated with liberalism since the days of President Franklin Roosevelt accept change in the future, or will it be associated with embracing the status quo because of its continual support of traditional Democratic programs such as strong unions, farm subsidies, welfare policies and other programs that polls indicate are losing public favor?

The Danger of Labeling

In the beginning of this viewpoint the reader was cautioned about the possibility of distortion from simplification. I would like

23

to also caution the reader about the danger of labeling a group or an individual as liberal, conservative, reactionary, or radical. A group may have what would be considered a liberal position on censorship of pornography but at the same time hold a conservative position of the question of defense spending. How would you then classify this group, right-wing or left-wing? Although a general conclusion may be reached about the positioning of a specific group on the political spectrum, one must always be careful about irrevocably labeling a group or an individual as reactionary, conservative, liberal, or radical. Individually, almost every person can be positioned at every stopping point on the political spectrum. One would have to conduct a long search to find a person who is a one hundred percent radical and demands a revolution for every cause or a liberal who is completely dissatisfied with the status quo. The search would be equally fruitless if one were to look for the complete conservative who is satisfied with everything as it is or the reactionary who wants to retreat totally into the past.

In spite of the danger of labeling it should not be avoided. When done with care and knowledge it can provide a helpful orientation for understanding issues of the day and the stances public figures take on them. After reading this viewpoint you might find it intriguing to take the political spectrum self-survey after viewpoint six in this chapter. Perhaps you already know. Are you a liberal or a conservative?

1. David Russell, "Political Spectrum Analogy," *Social Education*, October 1980, p. 519.

2. Pamela Johnston Conover and Stanley Feldman, "The Origins and Meanings of Liberal/Conservative Self-Identifications," *American Journal of Political Science*, Vol. 25, No. 4, November 1981, pp. 617-45.

3. Rexford G. Tugwell, *The Industrial Discipline and the Governmental Arts*, New York: Columbia University Press, 1934-5, p. 229.

4. In this hypothetical situation the reader must consider the need for a new train station and the method of building it open to question, otherwise the liberal solution would appear to be the only prudent one.

5. American government was partially founded on the conservative concept of direction for the masses by an enlightened minority. The founding fathers, while meeting at the Constitutional Convention in Philadelphia in 1787, made provisions for this practice in the new constitution. Various methods were devised to place the reins of government in the hands of the better educated and more responsible members of American society:
   1. The creation of the Senate as a check on the House of Representatives with members given six year terms to give them a greater degree of independence.
   2. The election of senators by state legislators rather than by the general voting public.
   3. The election of the President by electors rather than by the general voting public.

6. Russell Kirk, "Prescription, Authority and Ordered Freedom," *What Is Conservatism*, ed, Frank S. Meyer, New York: Holt, Rinehart & Winston, 1964, p. 27.

7. Ross J.S. Hoffman and Paul Levack, eds., *Burke's Politics: Selected Writings and Speeches of Edmund Burke*, New York: Alfred A. Knopf, 1949, p. 109.

"'Conservative' and 'liberal' . . . their descriptive utility is more and more limited in today's new political economy."

The Traditional Spectrum Is Obsolete

Kevin Phillips

Kevin Phillips is a syndicated columnist and CBS commentator who also publishes several newsletters and lectures widely. He is the publisher of *The American Political Report* and the author of five books, most recently *Post-Conservative America*. In the following viewpoint, Mr. Phillips argues that the traditional political spectrum, as presented in the preceding viewpoint, does not adequately describe the current American scene. He claims that the terms liberal and conservative came into common usage in the 19th century and have lost their descriptive utility in today's political economy. He calls for an overhaul of our political terminology, and he is not convinced that the fourfold description of the spectrum presented in viewpoint three provides the answer. What do you think of his evaluation?

As you read, consider the following questions:

1. Why does the author claim neither a twofold nor fourfold description of the political spectrum is accurate?
2. To what does he refer when using the term "reactionary liberalism"?
3. What difficulties does he predict in the years ahead for the coalition that elected Ronald Reagan in 1984?

Kevin Phillips, "Old Political Labels No Longer Fit," *The Wall Street Journal*, November 27, 1984. Reprinted with the author's permission.

Although the election dust has begun to settle around President Reagan's triumph, the result remains ambiguous in many respects. The outcome below the presidential level was mixed, as have been postelection analyses of the extent to which U.S. politics have been in a realignment process over the past 15 years. And we can also expect continuing confusion on a second dimension: ideological labels and semantics. However analysts strain to construe the outcome in conservative vs. liberal terms, the truth is far more complex. Indeed, the increasing failure of these two terms to describe the divisions and nuances of U.S. politics merits renewed attention, not least in interpreting Mr. Reagan's victory and the likely constituency clashes he will face during a second term.

In a new book, "Beyond Liberal and Conservative" (*Cato Institute*, 1984), University of Central Florida Profs. William Maddox and Stuart Lilie suggest that accurate political cataloguing really requires four terms: conservative, liberal, populist and libertarian. By their yardsticks, conservatives oppose government restraints on the economy, but favor social restraints. Liberals, of course, reverse these preferences. They favor government restrictions in the economic sector while opposing official restriction of social expression. Libertarians, in turn, oppose government regulation of the economy and personal behavior alike, while populists favor controls in both sectors. By the Lilie and Maddox measurements, populists and libertarians have emerged with as much political strength as the conservative and liberal camps—each of the four catagories has about 20% popular support with the voting public (the rest do not fit easily into any ideological box).

Various Ingredients

At the very least, the Lilie and Maddox reassessment of the political spectrum is a useful embellishment of an obsolete conservative-vs.-liberal dichotomy. In practice, though, the ideological fragmentation and confusion of American politics are so pervasive that this fourfold distinction won't solve matters either.

Let's begin with conservatism. One minor irony of 1984 is that support for the conservative Ronald Reagan probably encompasses a solid majority of populists and many libertarians as well. In part that's because Reaganism has its populist and libertarian as well as conservative ingredients. What's more, despite their partially incompatible outlooks as set forth below, the president has so far given all three constituencies something to cheer about as the accompanying table illustrates.

Straddling these divergences during the 1984 election campaign actually turned out to be rather easy for Mr. Reagan, at least once the Democrats rejected the candidate (Gary Hart) more oriented toward non-liberal constituencies in favor of Walter Mondale, a nominee whose ideology epitomizes special-interest politics or what I have called "reactionary liberalism." To many Americans, liberalism has lost its old identification with individualism and opportunity, standing instead for preferences for various groups and minorities: economic, sexual and racial. Populists, libertarians and conservatives alike disagree with this agenda.

Whether liberalism can rise above this linkage is a valid question. Officeholder after ex-liberal officeholder now prefers to be called something else—a progressive, usually. Surveys of state legislatures typically yield only a small minority of legislatiors willing to claim the liberal label. To prosper on the national level, then, the Democratic Party may need a metamorphosis of both ideological labels and outlooks.

Multiple Ideologies of the Reagan Constituency

Credo	Economic Philosophy	Social Philosophy
Present Reagan ideology	Limited intervention in the economy	Increasing intervention in morality
Libertarians	Minimal interventions in the economy	Minimal intervention in morality
Conservatives	Limited intervention in the economy	Substantial intervention in morality
Populists	Substantial intervention in the economy	Substantial intervention in morality

Yet conservatism, too, has its definitional problems. Much of what has been blithely called conservatism in recent years—the religious right, fundamentalist church doctrine, anti-abortion crusades, opposition to the federal judiciary and the Federal Reserve Board, the anti-tax movement, the anti-pornography rallies and the like—actually hails from the radical or populist streams of U.S. electoral history. What's more, "conservatism" is now stronger in the South and West, historically the country's populist and outsider regions.

All of this has created major difficulties for the genuinely conservative, Tory element in U.S. politics, especially the old Northeastern Yankee elite. Vice President George Bush personifies the discombobulation. The positions and manners Mr. Bush found it necessary to adopt in is debate with Geraldine Ferraro prompted New Right leader Richard Viguerie to congratulate him on having become a populist. At the same time, more gentrified commentators suggested he had become an embarrassment to Yale.

Over the next four years, relations among conservatives, populists and libertarians will undoubtedly become stickier. Once

27

the president can no longer brandish unifying opposition to Walter Mondale and reactionary liberalism, he will face policy choices certain to strain portions of his 1984 coalition. Because of the pressures of international economic competition, President Reagan's second term is likely to require more activist economic policies—setting out new guidelines and proposals in antitrust, trade policy, currency intervention, export promotion, encouragement of technology and the like. Some conservatives may not like that. Taxes may also be increased. At the same time, the president will probably continue to support the religious right's agenda on abortion, school prayer and general government intervention in the "moral sector."

To monitor the constituency impact of these trends without putting a new premium on distinctions among conservatives, libertarians and populists will be impossible. However, even there, a caveat is in order. If the label "conservative" is no longer all that useful, I'm not certain the "populist" and "libertarian" labels are all that helpful, either.

Consider that historically, a populist has been someone embracing government intervention in both the economic and moral sectors. Yet conservative populists now argue that populism has changed its stripes, that the average American now favors reducing, not increasing, the government role in the economy. By this thesis, economic deregulation, the movement toward a flat tax (eliminating government use of the tax code for public policy goals) and support for a gold standard (eliminating government manipulation of the currency) are all populist insofar as they seek to disestablish big government.

It's a partially plausible premise—the public is disenchanted with much of the growth in government's economic role—but an overall exaggeration. Realistically, what used to be called the George Wallace vote tends to applaud tax-revolt politicans and laugh at jokes about Washington bureaucrats on the one hand, while simultaneously approving expanded government programs in housing, road building, water resources, job retraining, protection of U.S. industry from unfair competition and so forth. Populism's old 19th-century definition may not be valid today, but the revisionist interpretation isn't either. Would that some new descriptive term emerge.

Changing Trends

So, too, with the notion of "libertarian" ideology. As an organized political party, the Libertarians have ebbed since 1980. However, conservative libertarianism has found some foothold in the small-government and deregulationist camps of the Reagan administration, and on a different and less intense ideological level of kindred preference for relatively minimal government intervention in economics and morality appeals to much of what came to be called the Yuppie vote in 1984.

Whether you call them neoliberals, young upwardly mobile professionals, brie-and-chablis progressives or whatever, the bulk of the relatively affluent voters who followed Eugene McCarthy in the late 1960s and early 1970s, John Anderson in 1980 and Gary Hart in 1984 combine a fair degree of economic "conservatism" (self-interest?) with a relatively permissive social and moral outlook. This is the growing electorate that will be offended if a second Reagan administration subsidizes steel on behalf of blue-collar Pennsylvania and proclaims fundamentalist Protestantism on behalf of rural South Carolina. Here, too, a new ideological label is in order.

What's more, because of the central changes overtaking America, both the populist and libertarian voting streams, as broadly defined, look like growth constituencies. At some risk of oversimplification, yesteryear's blue-collar liberal constituency has been reacting against cultural and economic change in a conservative populist direction, while the mushrooming ranks of affluent professionals have been diluting their conservatism with untraditional life styles and social values. Both trends are likely to continue.

Thus, to try to predict and analyze these 1985-88 stresses and strains in mere conservative vs. liberal terminology strikes me as confusing and counterproductive. The truth is that "conservative" and "liberal" are terms that came into common usuage only in the early 19th century following the French and Industrial revolutions, and their descriptive utility is more and more limited in today's new political economy. Like official indicators that bias federal economic data toward old manufacturing patterns and a smokestack yesteryear, our political nomenclature also needs an overhaul.

"The liberal-conservative dichotomy . . . is inadequate to describe and understand the opinions and behavior of the American people."

The Spectrum Has Four Positions

William S. Maddox & Stuart A. Lilie

William S. Maddox is associate professor of political science at the University of Central Florida. Stuart A. Lilie is associate professor and chairman of the department of political science at the same school. The following viewpoint is excerpted from a book published by The Cato Institute which describes itself as a libertarian research foundation. The authors claim that the orthodox definitions of liberal and conservative are no longer accurate. Rather than use the traditional two position description of the political spectrum, they suggest a two-dimensional approach, each with two basic positions. They would go beyond the use of the terms liberal and conservative, adding populist and libertarian, making a four-fold distinction.

As you read, consider the following questions:

1. Why do the authors think the political views of Americans cannot be accurately described by the terms liberal and conservative?
2. What rationale do they use to explain their four-way description of the spectrum based on the terms liberal, libertarian, populist, and conservative?

William S. Maddox and Stuart A. Lilie, *Beyond Liberal and Conservative*. Washington, DC: Cato Institute, 1984. Reprinted with permission.

Almost everyone finds public opinion and ideology in the United States confusing in some way. All too often analysts explain this confusion by concluding that the public itself is confused. It is our central argument that much of this confusion and misunderstanding stems from a simple fact: The liberal-conservative dichotomy (or even a liberal-moderate-conservative continuum) is inadequate to describe and understand the opinions and behavior of the American public. . . .

The Liberal-Conservative Dichotomy Is Inadequate

The class division on which ideological division historically has been based (the liberalism of the New Deal coalition versus Republican conservatism) no longer has the same meaning it once had and does not adequately explain the political behavior of the citizens. A person's economic standing is no longer a simple predictor of his ideology or voting behavior. As our economy changes from an industrial system to a service economy, the usual description of the occupational basis of ideological divisions between liberals and conservatives (blue collar versus white collar) no longer seems very useful. The accompanying increases in levels of educational attainment, mass media exposure to politics, and general affluence suggest that the class-based politics of liberal versus conservative, the "politics as usual" of the past, is not a very good description of what the public is thinking or doing ideologically.

Furthermore, political candidates often do not fit neatly into either a liberal or conservative mold, and the term "moderate" does not provide a very clear way to describe them either. Candidates themselves often reject these labels, although rarely do they offer us more informative summaries of their overall point of view. . . .

If Americans are ideological at all, the logic usually goes, they must be either liberal or conservative. If we find that they are not much of either of those, then the only ideological viewpoint that will describe them is something between those two extremes; in other words they are moderate.

Four-Way Description of Spectrum Is Preferable

It is our central thesis that the single liberal-conservative dichotomy—and the resulting two-way analysis of American politics—is inadequate for understanding belief systems or ideologies in the United States. Rather we think that mass belief systems are better understood if they are analyzed in terms of two separate dimensions—thereby making possible a four-way description of American politics. One dimension is attitude toward government intervention in the economy, and the other is attitude toward the maintenance or expansion of personal freedoms.

Different positions on government involvement in the economy

31

have generally been assumed to be the defining division between liberals and conservatives in contemporary America. However, the extent and nature of government regulation of personal behavior has also been an enduring conflict in American politics. We think that this conflict is both analytically and empirically distinct from conflict over the economic dimension. Other political scientists have recognized these two sets of issues and have surveyed public opinion on both dimensions; in doing so, though, they have still allowed for only two resulting ideological positions, liberal and conservative.

Figure 1

ISSUE DIMENSIONS AND IDEOLOGICAL CATEGORIES

		Government Intervention in Economic Affairs	
		For	Against
Expansion of Personal Freedoms	For	Liberal	Libertarian
	Against	Populist	Conservative

Our analysis uses these two issue dimensions—government economic intervention and expansion of personal freedoms—to define four rather than two ideological categories. We label these liberal, libertarian, populist, and conservative. Specifically the two dimensions combine as shown in figure 1. Liberals support government economic intervention and expansion of personal freedoms; conservatives oppose both. Libertarians support expanded individual freedom but oppose government economic intervention; populists oppose expansion of individual freedom but support government intervention in the economy. These four categories can be justified both theoretically and empirically. . . .

Analysis that begins by looking at two dimensions rather than one, and thereby uses four rather than two ideological categories, shows that a suprisingly large percentage of Americans have opinions on political issues that cohere in a consistent fashion and that can be seen as related to established traditions of Western political thought. The four categories we use here, therefore, are supported both by empirical evidence and by their relationship to traditions of political thought. . . .

Modern liberalism differs from its classical ancestor basically on the question of the proper relationship between government and the economy. The development of modern liberalism is in large part a response to the effects of industrialization in the 19th and 20th centuries. (Throughout the rest of this [viewpoint], "liberalism" will refer to modern liberalism.) Industrialization, while considered progressive by liberals, was associated with a great deal of change and dislocation. Increasing numbers of people lived in cities with the concomitant problems of congested housing and poor sanitation, and increasing numbers worked as wage laborers instead of as independent farmers or craftsmen. To many liberals the results seemed far removed from the autonomous, independent individual envisioned in the liberal ideal. Many reformers, such as the later John Stuart Mill and T.H. Green, began to reexamine the liberal argument that the state should not intervene in economic affairs. Green argued that there are circumstances in which government intervention, particularly in the economic realm, might actually promote rather than hinder individual development. These 19th-century thinkers began to support wage and hour laws and compulsory education, although other liberals viewed such regulations as unacceptable violations of the right of the individual to choose to work for whom and for whatever wage he wanted and the right of parents to educate their children as they saw fit.

Modifying Classical Liberalism

Attempts to regulate the business cycle were another source of modification of classical liberalism. While the first modification had been aimed more at individual welfare, this second one was an attempt to overcome the boom-and-bust business cycle, which reached its lowest point in the Great Depression of the 1930s. Liberals began to argue that government should attempt to slow expansion in boom periods and stimulate growth during recessions to even out the business cycle. The liberal theorist most associated with this view, of course, is John Maynard Keynes.

Modern liberals, while still valuing private property and the market, are willing to support government intervention to promote individual welfare and to regulate the economy. At the same time liberals argue fairly consistently that in terms of one's personal activity outside the economic realm, the individual should remain free of governmental restriction.

Modern liberalism in America has been closely associated with the dominant wing of the Democratic party. From the Great Depression era and the presidency of Franklin Roosevelt to the 1960s, such Democratic party leaders as Harry Truman, Adlai Stevenson, and John F. Kennedy made the basic principles of liberalism a cornerstone of most political debates. Since the Vietnam era, spokesmen such as Hubert Humphrey, George McGovern, and Edward Kennedy have carried on the liberal tradition but have often been divided over foreign policy issues. Today the principles of liberalism still are expressed primarily through Democratic party leaders and, on some issues, through spokesmen for civil rights groups or labor unions. Frustration with the results of liberal policies in the 1960s and 1970s has left liberalism an ideology on the defensive, often blamed for both economic dislocations and breakdowns in the moral order of our society. Although some liberals respond with what may be new variations or simply different labels, such as "progressive" or "neo-liberal," their commitment to civil liberties and government intervention in the economy remains intact.

Libertarianism

Libertarian thought represents a highly individualistic extension of classical liberalism into the 20th century. Libertarians explicitly embrace most of the assumptions of classical liberalism. Consequently most of the discussion of classical liberalism applies to libertarians as well. Until fairly recently people holding the belief that government should play a minimal role in both the economic realm and the realm of personal liberties have been called Manchester liberals, classical liberals, or libertarian conservatives. The establishment of the Libertarian party and its associated publicity, however, make "libertarian" a less confusing term than these.

Libertarians emphasize very strongly the autonomy of the individual and the minimal role required of government. A recent statement of libertarian philosophy says that "we hold that all individuals are unique . . . [and] we also believe that each individual human being is morally autonomous. . . ." Given that the rights of the individual are superior to all other political values, libertarians think that the individual should be free of government restraint in both economic and noneconomic spheres.

Property rights are central to individual rights; security and freedom in property transactions are prerequisites to individual development. Private property is seen as a liberating force, protecting the individual from arbitrary government intrusion. Libertarian thought opposes the economic interference of liberals on a variety of grounds. An unfettered market is more efficient than a regulated economy and therefore meets a greater variety of human needs. The truly needy can have their needs better met through private, voluntary action than through governmental programs. Further, need does not itself create a just claim to the property and wealth of others.

Property rights are necessary for human actualization, but it is also essential that the individual remain free of coercion in matters of religion, morality, conscience, and other purely private matters. Libertarians differ from their conservative colleagues in their rejection of government censorship and regulation of drugs and alcohol. Tolerance of individual differences is a crucial point in libertarian thought. Libertarians think that maximum individual choice in both economic and noneconomic realms can be achieved only if the individual is free from government interference.

In times of major economic crisis (the Great Depression, for example) or international problems (World War II or the East-West tensions that followed), the libertarian concern with issues of personal freedom has not been articulated in American politics. Several factors have changed this in recent years: a more politically conscious citizenry exposed to more education and mass media, increased affluence of a large middle class, the polarization of the two major parties into "liberal" Democrats versus "conservative" Republicans, and the inability of either ideology to deal with some continuing political problems. Thus we have begun to see some expression of libertarian views recently through individual leadership, the Libertarian party, and what has been erroneously called the "liberal" wing of the Republican party. Even such mainstream political figures as Jerry Brown, Barber Conable, John Anderson, and Gary Hart have described themselves or have been described as fiscally conservative and socially liberal—which is roughly our definition of libertarianism, albeit in a very mild form. . . .

IDEOLOGICAL COMPOSITION OF PARTY IDENTIFIERS IN 1980

Democrats	Liberals 30%	Populists 37%	Cons. 11%	Libt. 7%	Divided & Inattentive 15%

Republicans	Liberals 13% / Populists 18%	Conservatives 27%	Libertarians 29%	Divided & Inattentive 13%

Independents	Liberals 25%	Populists 20%	Cons. 17%	Libertarians 23%	Divided & Inattentive 15%

Source: CPS.

Conservatism

Conservatism is perhaps the most confusing of our four ideological categories. One source of confusion is the frequent use of the term as a defense of the status quo, especially as a rationalization for a particular set of property arrangements. Another source is that those contemporary Americans who call themselves conservative have also often been strident nationalists, thus bringing into American conservatism points of view not entirely consistent with the term's historical meaning. Popular perceptions and use of the term are also confusing. Conservatism has been associated with support for all basic American values, attachment to big business, religious approaches to politics, and general closed-mindedness, as well as with what we describe below as populism. Traditional Burkean or "organic" conservatism developed out of the European feudal tradition and has not been a prevalent philosophy in the United States. Elements of this philosophy, though, do underlie much of American conservatism. Organic conservatism takes society, not the individual, as the fundamental entity to be protected and enhanced. Conservatives view the "autonomous individual" as a fiction. The individual can exist only in society, and is defined by society.

This kind of conservatism takes a pessimistic view of human nature, believing that humans, marred by original sin, are prone to be selfish and in need of moral guidance. Left to his own devices, man is dangerous. Human action needs to be restrained, guided in accordance with correct principles. Religion, natural law, right reason, and tradition are important sources of such principles. Government's function is to interpret and enforce these correct principles through law, thus ensuring justice and civility through the use of authority.

As societies evolve slowly, a given society represents centuries of accumulated widom, which is embodied in the society's traditional norms and institutional arrangements. Conservatives stress authority, seeing true freedom as possible only within an ordered society that guides and limits the baser human instincts. Without authority, the human individual is confused, alone, and likely to rebel and destroy his heritage of complex social and political institutions. Because they see inherited social and political institutions and established social patterns as so very important, and because they distrust human nature, conservatives believe that governmental power must be used to regulate individual choices in many areas that the liberal or libertarian would leave unfettered. What political observer Kevin Phillips calls "post-conservatism" is the contemporary manifestation of the basic conservative claim that a commitment to traditional values, such as religion and economic freedom, together with limits on personal behavior, is necessary to preserve society and therefore the individual.

Skeptical Conservatives

Conservatives are highly skeptical of people's ability to correctly analyze the complexity of historically developed society, and thus are highly skeptical of people's capacity for correctly planning for or bringing about desirable economic conditions. Attempts to impose "rational" plans on an organically evolved society are almost certainly doomed to failure, or at least to produce unforeseen, undersirable consequences. Because they see human capacity as limited, conservatives oppose the use of government power to

36

regulate economic affairs. European conservatives have not been as trusting of a free market, or of business, as their American counterparts, but conservatives generally see economic inequality as the natural consequence of inequality of human ability and energy. Attempts to counteract this natural inequality lead to the loss of initiative and excellence, which many conservatives see as having occurred in the United States. For these reasons conservatives see a need to use government power to guide and limit human behavior in the realm of individual morals, but at the same time oppose the use of government to restrict human behavior in the economic realm.

From the defeat of Herbert Hoover in 1932 to the election of Ronald Reagan in 1980, these conservative ideas functioned primarily as the "loyal opposition" to liberalism in the United States. An occasional spokesman, such as Robert Taft, Everett Dirksen, or Barry Goldwater, stood out, but conservative views rarely caught the public's attention at the national level or even dominated one major political party. The association of conservatism with big business or the rich probably had much to do with this, as did the tendency for the public to talk as conservatives at the abstract level ("government is too big") but act like liberals when they wanted a particular benefit from government. Furthermore, the advancement of conservative thought in contemporary politics had been hindered by a tendency toward ideological infighting among its supporters. The 1980 Republican presidential nomination race, for example, often centered around which potential candidate was the most "pure" conservative.

Displeased Critics

Some of President Reagan's harshest critics have been conservatives displeased by his shifts from ideological purity. Two situations probably explain much of this displeasure. First, the immense size of government activity, increasing dependence on government, and such "uncontrollable" budget items as Social Security mean that conservatism's ideal of minimal economic activity cannot be achieved without drastic changes in the national economy and all citizens' lives. Therefore conservatives must compromise one of their basic tenets; how much and what to compromise is then a matter of intense debate. Second, the commitment to nonintervention in the economy is also confused by the capitalist system's connection with government. Conservatives see capitalism as essential for social stability, but modern capitalism is inextricably linked with and benefits from government action— tax loopholes, government contracts, price supports, and protection from foreign competition, for example. Thus the conservatives' belief in nonintervention often is not compatible with their support of business in today's mixed economy. It is this type of

37

dilemma that leads a conservative such as Karl Hess to abandon that point of view and move toward libertarianism.

Populism

This fourth ideological category is in some ways the most difficult to identify in that "populism" is a term with a varied and largely historical meaning. Populism has been associated more with political protest and political action than with theoretical writings. Indeed, populists have often mistrusted intellectuals and their elaborate theories, so that the literature associated with populism is relatively small compared to that on the other ideologies discussed here.

SUMMARY OF SOCIAL AND DEMOGRAPHIC TENDENCIES OF
IDEOLOGICAL TYPES IN 1980

LIBERALS	LIBERTARIANS
Under age 41 (66%)	Under age 41 (55%)
Some college and college degree	Advanced and college degree
All income levels	Middle to high income
Strongest in West and Northeast	Strongest in West
84% white	Middle class
Slightly more females	96% white
More Jewish and "no religion"	More "no religion"
POPULISTS	CONSERVATIVES
New Deal generation and older	Fifties generation or older
High school diploma or less (83%)	All educational levels
Below $10,000/year income	Middle to upper income
Southern and Midwestern	Strongest in Midwest
Working class	96% white
24% nonwhite	
Slightly more females	
Slightly more Catholic	

Populists favor government intervention in the economy to benefit the "average man" or "little guy." Populists are not anticapitalist; they accept most of the assumptions of liberalism, especially emphasing individualism, equality of opportunity, and property rights. Their protest is that the liberal, capitalist system has not provided these values for a large enough number of people. The system has been perverted or misused, and government must act to correct these abuses. Large corporations, especially railroads, banks and other financial institutions (and more recently multinational corporations), and the politicians who collaborate with them

38

must be regulated so that the market economy can function properly. With an appropriate level of economic regulation, directed by an appropriate set of politicians who respond to the needs of ordinary people, a free-market economy will function properly to provide a wider distribution of private property. While many populists today live in cities, they still retain an identification with a simpler, less urban society. Their ideal remains the independent, landowning farmer (in this they draw from Thomas Jefferson and Andrew Jackson), the small businessman, and perhaps the wage earner—people living in small towns or rural areas.

Rural Support

The populist political movement that culminated in the People's Party of the 1890s had its greatest support in the rural areas of the Midwest and South (many of today's self-proclaimed populists, such as Fred Harris, Barry Commoner, and George Wallace are also from these areas). Populism is the most explicitly mass-based of the ideological categories discussed here. Distrusting bigness and centralization, populists also tend to distrust the social and moral changes they see as a manifestation of bigness and centralization. They look backward to a time when life was simpler. This desire for a return to the simplicity of an imagined past is the basis for the moralism and at times ethnocentrism—and racism—of populism. In their search for an explanation as to why a liberal, capitalist system has not lived up to its promise, populists have sometimes blamed "foreigners," "Catholics," "pointy-headed bureaucrats," or "humanists," as well as giant corporations. Traditional social and moral values are an important part of the lost past, and populists are willing, sometimes eager, to use governmental power to establish or reestablish the traditional values of rural American life.

> For all the Southern Populists, financial reformers and an timonopoly greenbackers alike, the proper society bore a great resemblance to the rural, agricultural communities in which most of them lived or had grown up. . . . While individual economic competition and the market system for the most part went unchallenged, personal relationships and moral and religious precepts more importantly than Adam Smith's invisible hand and the local police force appeared to delineate and guide the social and economic life of the community. (Bruce Palmer, *Man Over Money: The Southern Populist Critique of American Capitalism*, 1980.)

Thus populists support government regulation of the economy to prevent concentrations of wealth and to ensure a more equal distribution of private property—but not to destroy private property or capitalism. At the same time they support the use of governmental power to regulate individual behavior so that it conforms to traditional moral and social values.

The expression of populist views in American politics was probably clearest almost a century ago with the third-party movements of the late 19th century. Since then the dominance of economic issues has led many populists to support such liberal leaders as Franklin D. Roosevelt. . . . The populist point of view has been most evident in national politics with the emergence of a particularly colorful spokesman, a George Wallace or Huey Long for example. It is difficult to define a modern populist movement when the populist name is claimed by politicans ranging from Fred Harris and Barry Commoner to George Wallace and Richard Viguerie. Perhaps, though, it could be argued that these apparently diverse figures ultimately have much in common: hostility to established interests, a desire to use government to enforce their own moral and economic beliefs, and a greater distrust of classical liberal values than is found among either liberals or conservatives. The moralist emphasis of the New Right sometimes seems to reflect populist assumptions. In the daily workings of politics, however, populism seems to be a guiding philosophy for quite a few congressmen. An ideology that is difficult to simplify or identify, populism is also difficult to use as a basis for leadership or organized movements, despite its preeminence as a belief system for many Americans.

Conclusion

We have described four major ideological categories, in terms of their philosophical views and how they relate to questions of governmental economic intervention and the expansion of personal freedoms. . . .We do not maintain that the segments of the public we classify as libertarian, liberal, conservative, and populist do in fact hold these complex philosophical positions. Nonetheless we can say that their positions are consistent with these well-established systems of thought and therefore should not be considered nonideological or inconsistent.

*"The preponderance of voters holds a mixture
of conservative, moderate, and liberal views."*

The Spectrum Has
Eight Positions

James L. Sundquist

James L. Sundquist is a senior fellow in the Brookings Governmental Studies Program at the Brookings Institution. The following viewpoint is taken from a Brookings' book, *Dynamics of the Party System*, which analyzed historical changes and recent trends in America's political party system. In evaluating the Reagan presidency and its impact on America's party system, Mr. Sundquist uses an eight-position grouping of liberals and conservatives to help explain the coalition that gave the Republicans a majority in the 1980 and 1984 elections. He believes this eight-position breakdown of political perspectives provides a more accurate appraisal of the American electorate than the two traditional labels of liberal and conservative.

As you read, consider the following questions:

1. What rationale does the author use in dividing the American electorate into eight groups?
2. Using the author's groupings, where would you place your state's two senators? Where would you place yourself?

James L. Sundquist, *Dynamics of the Party System*. Washington, DC: The Brookings Institution, 1983. Reprinted with permission.

The New Right-Reagan strategy brought a host of devoted, zealous converts to the Republican cause. But the traditional, intuitive, compromising strategy of political parties in the United States does have its basis in experience and common sense—and therein lay the special weakness of the Reagan coalition. For coming down sharply on one side or the other of a divisive issue repels at the same time it attracts. When the Republican party in 1976 for the first time took decisive stands in its platform against busing, abortion, gun control, affirmative-action hiring quotas, and for school prayer, it increased the number of voters who were crosspressured, who agreed with the GOP position on some issues but prefered the Democratic position—or Democratic ambiguity—on others. . . .

Eight Positions on Three Public Issues

The nature of the crosspressures, and the dilemmas they present to the Reagan coalition, can be illustrated by dividing the electorate into eight groups determined by whether voters are liberal (L) or conservative (C) on each of three separable policy dimensions:*

Eight Possible Positions

	Group							
	1	2	3	4	5	6	7	8
Domestic economic and role-of-government issues	L	L	L	L	C	C	C	C
Social and moral issues	L	L	C	C	L	L	C	C
Foreign and military issues	L	C	L	C	L	C	L	C

The grouping disregards, of course, persons whose views may be unfixed, inconsistent, or borderline. But among those whose views may be categorized as either conservative or liberal, an individual may be to the left of center on one set of issues and to the right on another. A Republican who joined his party because he opposed Democratic policies leading to bigger government and higher spending does not necessarily adopt a hard-line antidetente stand with accompanying high military expenditures—the Reagan-New Right definition of foreign policy and military conservatism. Nor does a conservative position on fiscal and economic policy oblige its holder to be against the equal rights amendment, in favor of outlawing abortion, and opposed to any form of gun control. Even within each of the issue complexes, of course, a citizen may be conservative on one question and liberal on another, though the probability of consistency of views is greater within the issue complexes than among them.

Group 8 (CCC) thus includes voters who are conservative on all three types of issues; President Reagan clearly belongs in this group. At the other extreme are the voters in group 1 (LLL), who are liberal on all issues; George McGovern may be chosen as the prototype. In between are those who are conservative on some issues and liberal on others. While public figures are given to straddling crosscutting issues whenever they can, making them difficult to classify in any simplified matrix such as this one, some names can be suggested for illustrative purposes. Thus Senators Henry M. Jackson of Washington and Daniel P. Moynihan of New York, traditional liberals on role-of-government issues but conservatives on foreign and military policy and perhaps on some social issues, would find themselves in group 2 (LLC) or 4 (LCC). Vice President George Bush, who has earned the suspicion of the New Right because of a liberal stand on some social issues, might be in group 6 (CLC) rather than group 8. Moderate Republican senators such as Bob Packwood of Oregon and Lowell P. Weicker, Jr., of Connecticut would probably belong in group 5 (CLL), and a few on the party's liberal fringe might even be placed in group 1 (LLL), taking their place there with the liberal wing of the Democratic party. The "populist" element of the New Right, fully committed to government action on behalf of working men and women, small farmers, and small business but conservative on other issues, has its place in group 4 (LCC).

Becoming a Majority Party

The same forces of public opinion that propelled President Reagan into office have also pressed voters and political leaders to the right in recent yers, and the CCCs have grown in number. They no doubt represent, in the 1980s, substantially more than one-eighth of the total electorate, but there is no evidence in public opinion data that they are anywhere near a majority. From all the survey evidence, the preponderance of voters holds a mixture of conservative, moderate, and liberal views, with a strong tendency toward ambivalence. For the Republican party to become the majority party in the country, then, it must attract the allegiance of substantial numbers from the six groups made up of the crosspressured individuals who are committed neither to conservatism nor to liberalism on the entire range of public issues.

*This eight-category grouping was first presented, with slightly different terminology and with the groups numbered in reverse order, in James L. Sundquist and Richard M. Scammon, "The 1980 Election: Profile and Historical Perspective," in Ellis Sandoz and Cecil V. Crabb, Jr., eds., *A Tide of Discontent: The 1980 Elections and Their Meaning* (Congressional Quarterly Press, 1981), pp. 30-31. Frank Whelon Wayman and Ronald R. Stockton, "The Structure and Stability of Political Attitudes: Findings from the 1974-1976 Dearborn Panel Study," paper prepared for the annual meeting of the American Political Science Association, 1980, esp. p. 9, found in a study of 800 voters in one Michigan city that the social issues were indeed crosscutting. They found social and cultural liberalism or conservatism was essentially unconnected with economic liberalism or conservatism, as these terms had been defined since the New Deal. Of the two "distinct" attitude clusters, economic views were related to, and reinforced, partisan identification, but social-cultural views were basically unrelated to partisanship and disruptive of the established political alignment.

"A conservative accepts man's inequalities as part of his heritage and considers liberty and property to have priority over equality."

A Conservative Views the Spectrum

George A. Reimann

George A. Reimann is a conservative writer and a former vice president of the Tennessee Rifle Association. He believes that the key to understanding the ideas of liberalism and conservatism lies in historical analysis of the terms. The following viewpoint, originally entitled "A Rational Explanation," presents such an analysis.

As you read, consider the following questions:

1. According to Mr. Reimann, how do liberals differ from conservatives?
2. How did Rousseau, Marx, Shaw, and Burke contribute to the concepts of liberalism and conservatism?
3. What conclusion does the author present?

George A. Reimann, "A Rational Explanation." Reprinted from *Life Lines*, Vol. 14, No. 24, February 25, 1972.

When the terms "Liberalism" and "Conservatism" are bandied about, it is evident that few Americans fully comprehend the concepts associated with these terms. The dictionary yields: Liberalism—favorable to progress or reform, as in political or religious reform; noting or pertaining to a political party advocating measures of progressive political reform; Conservatism—noting or pertaining to a political party whose characteristic principle is opposition to change in the institutions of a country. Boiled down to the residue, Liberalism equals innovation and Conservatism equals opposition. Satisfied?

An encyclopedia may be more enlightening, but here the emphasis is not on any uniqueness of American Liberalism and Conservatism, but on their histories. And as the evolution of these philosophies is traced, the trail grows colder as it nears the present time. A lingering impression persists of innovation vs. opposition, or good guys against bad guys.

Liberal Origins

Now it's our turn, and if you have already wagered that liberals will come in second, you can collect now. The term "liberal" stems from the word "liberalis"—pertaining to a free man. "Free man" in the context of current American Liberalism is largely based upon the philosophical theories of Jean-Jacques Rousseau (1712-1778). Rousseau did not invent Liberalism, however, he was an author and political theorist of considerable intellect and his philosophical forays included advocacy of popular sovereignty and a theory of democratic government. But having given credit where it was due, it must be observed that Rousseau became increasingly alienated from the established social and political order of his time. His "Discourse on the Origin and Bases of Inequality Among Men" (1754) indicted the political state and the concept of private property while it glorified "natural man." As Rousseau saw it, "natural man" was inherently good and feelings and emotions were the "primary values" in life. But natural man's primary values were corrupted by his own relationships, his institutions, and his environment. Civilization itself was to blame for man's impressive inventory of vices. . . .

Marx and Shaw

One is reluctant to invite Karl Marx into a critique of Liberalism, for to do so is to cause hysterical howls of indignant protest which drown out all subsequent discussion. Yet Karl Marx must enter, even if uninvited. Marx was one of many convinced of man's inherent goodness, believing that when the victims of capitalism, the working class, overthrew the owning class by violent revolution, wisdom and justice would miraculously accrue to the workers, thereby enabling them to rule the world beneficently. Marx concluded: "Qualities of human intelligence, personality,

emotional and religous life merely reflect man's economic environment. The evil man is just a reflection of his environment." Thus,
if man's environment were corrected, his nature would
automatically transform so that he would work according to his
ability and desire to receive only according to his needs.
The Fabian Socialists organized in 1884, a year after Marx's
death. The Fabians planned to reorganize society by gradually
transferring control of property and capital from individuals to
the "community" for the "general benefit," thereby establishing
a socialistic, one-world order. George Bernard Shaw, a Fabian
founder and its most articulate spokesman, endorsed Marx's Utopian concept of compulsory equality of condition but deplored
open class warfare and violent revolution. . . .
So the Fabians began working for change by indoctrinating the
young scholars. Eventually, they believed, these "intellectual"
revolutionaries would acquire great power and influence in the
opinion making and power wielding agencies of the world. In practice it meant slow, piecemeal changes in established concepts of
morality, law, government, economics, and education. The Fabians
rejected all suggestions that they form their own party, preferring to impose their influence and to change everything by administrative infiltration of existing educational institutions,
political parties, civil service, etc. Salvation by subterfuge! . . .

Liberal Myths

I suppose I am still a liberal within the original meaning of that
much abused word, although having learned through experience
more than is dreamed of in the philosophy of most Western liberals,
I no longer share their faith in the inevitability of progress and the
perfectability of man through the creation of a better material
environment.

Freda Utley in her *Odyssey of a Liberal.*

Liberalism is said to have matured in America during the social
and economic changes wrought by the industrial revolution in the
19th century. Free enterprise and self reliance were in high esteem.
Relative to earlier times, a high degree of individual liberty and
freedom of action were achieved. But things were far from perfect.
Inequalities and injustice were still evident everywhere in various
forms. Liberals of that time brought pressure to bear on government to restrict individual freedom where it appeared to cause
inequality. But inequality persisted. Answer: More coercive
government control. . . .
Were the definition of Conservatism restricted to its being the
opposite (or opposition) of Liberalism, then the preceding text

47

might pass as a definition, with apologies for indicating what something is by describing what it is not. But such a restriction assumes the pre-existence of Liberalism in order that Conservatism may rise to oppose it when in fact Conservatism signifies the established order which Liberalism seeks to change.

Scholars credit Edmund Burke (1729-1797) with laying the foundation for modern Conservative thought. Burke's philosophy does not lend itself readily to a summary, and a condensation risks injustice. Burke held to Christian theology and morality in expressing a coherent view of social order based on natural law. He believed that to achieve liberty and justice, a government must be in harmony with historical experience; that an enduring government is a contract of the eternal society, a willing obligation to the dead, the living, and those yet unborn. A viable government is not an artificial contrivance of the intellectual whims of the moment. Individuals are foolish but the species is wise, and the wisdom of the species, the natural aristocracy, should govern, preserving the method of nature in the conduct of the state, while blending the best of the old order into the changes required for society's survival.

Conservatism extends beyond Burke's view of the proper relationship between the government and the governed. Conservative tenets recognize that men are unequal in terms of ambition, ability, intelligence, and character; that human reason is prone to error, of limited reach, and often governed by emotion; that liberty takes precedence over equality, so that one cannot infringe upon the liberty of another in the name of equality; and that one must be free to choose between right and wrong and accept responsibility for the consequences of his actions. . . .

Conclusion

To summarize, a Liberal strives to achieve equality among men and believes that inequalities result from factors in man's environment. Various "unfavorable" experiences during a lifetime cause a person to misbehave. If a suitable environment were devised (presumably by the government), man would cease being such a difficult creature and would become instead equal and agreeable. A Conservative accepts man's inequalities as part of his heritage and considers liberty and property to have priority over equality. Man must be free to make his own choices, not intrude into the affairs of others, and be responsible for his actions. Government should be guided by the sure footing of proven philosophies, and minimize its control over one's private affairs by functioning only to maintain the order and justice required to perpetuate a well-organized society.

"It is time to end the futile quarrel between 'liberals' . . . and conservatives. . . . We are all liberals, we are all conservatives."

A Liberal Views the Spectrum

Henry Steele Commager

Henry Steele Commager is one of America's leading liberal historians. The author of numerous books (*The American Mind, The Empire of Reason,* and others), he regularly contributes scholarly articles and editorials to prominent publications throughout the country. In the following viewpoint, he shows why political labeling can be misleading. In identifying the common threads that make up American liberalism and conservatism, he reminds conservatives of the unifying heritage that all Americans share.

As you read, consider the following questions:

1. List Commager's seven distinguishing features of liberalism.
2. What point does the author make in discussing Alexander Hamilton?
3. According to Commager, how do liberals differ from conservatives?

Henry Steele Commager, "Liberalism, Conservatism Are Two Sides of the Same American Coin," *Los Angeles Times,* December 3, 1979. Reprinted with the author's permission.

Recently the National Conservative Political Action Committee placed a full page advertisement critical of Sen. Edward M. Kennedy, D-Mass., in newspapers throughout the United States. It asked the following question of the American people: "What makes you think that an extreme liberal is able to make a good president?" It is astonishing that the term liberal is now a dirty word.

What is meant by liberalism?

The word "liberal" comes from the same root-word as does the word "liberty"—the Latin *liber,* which means "free." Its repudiation by modern conservatives constitutes a failure to understand the historical roots of conservatism as well as a failure to understand the nature of liberalism.

Those who use the terms liberal and liberalism in a pejorative sense would do well to consult dictionaries, American and English alike, for enlightenment. All give the same definitions: a liberal is one who is "free from prejudice;" who "supports religious freedom and the right to dissent;" who is "favorable to changes and reforms leading in the direction of freedom and democracy;" who is "tolerant of the ideas of others;" or who is "generous and open-hearted." In the headlong retreat from liberalism are we now to commit ourselves to intolerance, prejudice and conformity? Historically, the "liberal arts" are those worthy of "free men;" are we to turn now to those studies that are not fit for free men?

As those and a score of other definitions make clear, liberalism is not a particular program but rather a philosophical attitude.

The Features of Liberalism

What are the distinguishing features of that liberalism that have now become so fashionable to regard with suspicion?

First, a passion for what Thomas Jefferson called the "illimitable freedom of the human mind" and an "uncompromising hostility to every form of tyranny over the minds of men," whether that be political, religious or military.

Second, a repudiation of the tyranny of ignorance, of poverty and of vice, because these deny or inhibit the exercise of true freedom.

Third, a faith in reason and in the ability of men to govern themselves when their minds are liberated by education and their judgments protected by the orderly processes of the law.

Fourth, respect for the dignity of every individual—a respect that requires equal rights and equal justice in law and society.

Fifth, an acceptance of the will of the majority as long as that will operates under the law, with respect for the rights and interests of minorities.

Sixth, a commitment to the principle that the earth belongs to the living, not the dead, and that while we have an obligation to

Two Fine Words

Liberal vs. conservative—what really is meant by those two words?

An old and respected friend of mine thinks he knows the difference. He calls himself a conservative. He goes white in the face and splutters when he has to use the hated word "liberal." His intensity is such that you would almost think he was a Roman Catholic speaking of Protestants, or vice versa, back in days of the religious wars when they joyfully burned each other at the stake, singing hymns the while. But when asked to identify what he means by "liberal" he only says, "someone who enjoys spending other people's money."

What do people who think of themselves as "liberals" mean when they spit out the word "conservative" with equal intensity? They mean someone totally selfish who cares nothing for the community as a whole, but solely about what he can take from the system.

What a pity that two fine words, liberal and conservatives, have been so debased and distorted in American political usage. Conservative once meant a person concerned about preserving the best in the social and political heritage. It did not mean and certainly should not mean a layer of rich and powerful who use public office largely for their own selfish, personal or class profit. Edmund Burke thought he was being conservative when he spoke out in Parliament against measures intended to coerce the fractious American colonists. Benjamin Disraeli thought he was being conservative when he introduced legislation to reduce and eventually prohibit such monstrous things as children being used to pull carts in coal mines.

Liberal once meant to favor a free, marketplace economy. It meant freedom from government intrusion into and management of the marketplace. It meant the right of the industrious merchant or manufacturer to invest his money as he chose. It meant the opposite of everything that happens in either a fascist or a communist society.

Many Americans who now call themselves conservatives would be liberals under the older meaning of the word. Most American liberals are conservative in the sense that they care about the welfare and the happiness of the American people, who are, after all, the country's most valuable asset. To try to conserve their health and increase their productivity is properly speaking, a conservative thing to do.

Joseph C. Harsch, "Liberals vs. Conservatives," July 22, 1976. Reprinted by permission from *The Christian Science Monitor*© 1976 The Christian Science Publishing Society All Rights Reserved.

preserve what is best in the past, our primary fiduciary obligation is to posterity.

Seventh, the Jeffersonian belief—a belief that animated the generation of the Founding Fathers—that people have an inalienable right to pursue and obtain happiness.

It will not escape those familiar with American history that much of this agenda is also the agenda of conservatism. In the United States, liberalism and conservatism have been, from the beginning, two sides of the same coin, and our greatest liberals—Thomas Jefferson, Abraham Lincoln and Franklin D. Roosevelt—also have been our greatest conservatives.

The Foundations of Conservatism

Conservatism, as defined by its philosophical father Edmund Burke, rested on three foundations: the monarchy, the church and tradition. Liberalism, as explained by John Stuart Mill and Herbert Spencer, meant that government should keep its hands off the social and economic activities of its citizens and content itself with keeping order and enforcing the law. As Spencer put it, government should be "anarchy plus the policeman."

Though many of our modern conservatives still accept Burke's philosophy, they also accept the liberal concept of government as umpire. Neither view has anything whatever to do with the American experience. Because America had no monarchy, no church and little tradition, its citizens could give a different and more sensible meaning to conservatism. In America, conservatism has sought to conserve the natural resources of soil, water, forests and air; to conserve, and prosper, the dignity of every individual man and woman so that they could enjoy to the fullest that liberty and equality which Nature and God had bestowed upon them, and to conserve that heritage of arts, science, religion and law that we call civilization. . . .

Conservatives Should Look to the Past

It would not be necessary to remind even the most purblind conservatives of all if they knew their own history—which they do not. They inextricably link the history of conservatism with that of the Republican Party, forgetting that the Grand Old Party has often tried to be a government of the people. Most conservatives have forgotten that Alexander Hamilton, the spiritual father of both conservatism and the Republican Party, was the most ardent champion of a strong central government in our entire history; and they have forgotten that it was Hamilton who asserted that "all the underground wealth" belonged, as a matter of course, to the national government "to be disposed of by Congress as it saw fit for the best interests of the nation." They have forgotten, too, that it was the first Republican Party that *liberated* the slaves, and wrote into the Constitution the 14th

Amendment that quite effectively legally legitimized governmental centralization.

They choose not to remember that in the golden age of conservative politics—the age of Theodore Roosevelt, Elihu Root, Albert Beveridge and William Howard Taft—it was the Republican Party that maintained a government powerful enough to intervene aggressively in the domestic economy and in world affairs. By insisting on a hard and fast division between conservatives and liberals, between Republicans and Democrats, many of today's conservatives ignore the fact that since President Woodrow Wilson's administration the two parties have wrestled themselves into each other's clothes. . . .

Conclusion

In his first inaugural address, given in 1801, Thomas Jefferson said, "We are all republicans." We should heed his words. It is time to end the futile quarrel between "liberals" (who often demonstrate as little awareness of their own history as do "conservatives"), and conservatives. If our society is to recover the unity that it must have to survive, it must recognize that we are all Democrats, we are all Republicans, we are all federalists, we are all nationalists, we are all liberals, we are all conservatives.

Political Spectrum Self-Survey

Most people probably never reflect carefully on their personal political orientation. They rarely think of themselves in terms of being a liberal or a conservative. Have you? What label would you apply to yourself? Are you a liberal or a conservative? This exercise provides an opportunity for you to determine your position on the political spectrum.

Consider each of the twenty statements that follow. Circle the number after each statement that best represents your position. After you have completed all twenty statements, add up your score. Are you a liberal, a moderate, or a conservative?

5 = agree strongly, 4 = agree, 3 = undecided,
2 = disagree, 1 = disagree strongly

1. The United States must maintain strong ties with right-wing dictatorships to stop the spread of communism   5   4   3   2   1

2. An amendment, outlawing abortion, should be added to the Constitution.   5   4   3   2   1

3. A time for voluntary, silent prayer should be a part of the public school curriculum.   5   4   3   2   1

4. The United States must do all in its power to topple the communist government in Nicaragua.   5   4   3   2   1

5. A unilateral nuclear freeze by the United States would endanger its security.   5   4   3   2   1

6. The federal government should not interfere with handgun sales.   5   4   3   2   1

7. State governments should use the death penalty more frequently to deter violent criminals.   5   4   3   2   1

54

8. The United States must stop the spread 5 4 3 2 1
of communism, wherever it occurs in the
world.

9. Federal environmental laws are too harsh, 5 4 3 2 1
restricting needed economic growth.

10. Military spending, although burdensome, 5 4 3 2 1
must be increased to keep pace with
inflation.

11. Welfare programs have become too 5 4 3 2 1
expensive and have created a dependent
underclass. Welfare expenditures must be
reduced.

12. The United States must develop a "star 5 4 3 2 1
wars" defense system, regardless of the
cost.

13. The size of the federal bureaucracy must 5 4 3 2 1
be greatly reduced.

14. Communism is the greatest danger 5 4 3 2 1
facing the United States.

15. Federal funding of abortions for people 5 4 3 2 1
on welfare should be stopped.

16. An equal rights amendment to the 5 4 3 2 1
Constitution would be unnecessary and
unwise.

17. The federal government should encourage 5 4 3 2 1
the development of nuclear power to
preserve resources and reduce the balance
of payments deficit.

18. Secular humanism has had a disastrous 5 4 3 2 1
effect on public morality.

19. Equal opportunity laws are unfair 5 4 3 2 1
to the majority of Americans.

20. The Defense Department is unnecessarily 5 4 3 2 1
criticized by Americans who could use a
dose of patriotism.

liberal	moderate liberal	moderate	moderate conservative	conservative
(20-35)	(36-51)	(52-68)	(69-84)	(85-100)

Periodical Bibliography

The following list of periodical articles deals with the subject matter of this chapter.

Commentary
"What Is a Liberal—Who Is a Conservative?" September 1976.

Joseph Epstein
"True Virtue," *New York Times Magazine*, November 24, 1985.

Marshall Fritz
"A True Political Spectrum," *Libertarian Party News*, Spring 1986.

Kenneth E. John & Christine Russell
"Americans' Political Views Have Not Become More Conservative," *Washington Post National Weekly Edition*, March 25, 1985.

John McLaughlin
"What's New with Neos?" *National Review*, March 28, 1986.

Thomas Moore
"The New Libertarians Make Waves," *Fortune*, August 5, 1985.

The New Republic
"Neoliberals, Paleoliberals," April 9, 1984.

George Seldes
"'Liberal'—A New Dirty Word," *The Churchman*, November 1981.

Daniel Seligman
"Political Pigeonholes," *Fortune*, December 24, 1984.

2 CHAPTER

What Are the Roots of the Political Spectrum?

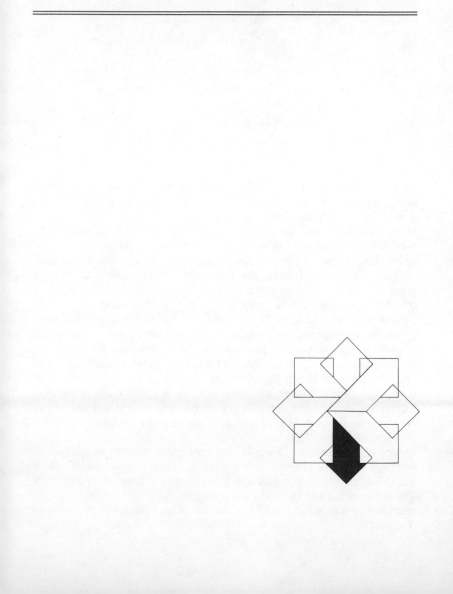

Chapter Preface

This chapter offers what the editors believe is a representative sampling of ideas from which much of the modern political spectrum derives. Included are excerpts from the works and speeches of both political philosophers and practical politicians. It is significant that the authors' opinions on government are largely based upon their views of human nature as revealed by history and experience. Thomas Hobbes, for example, believing that all people are self-seeking, egocentric, and forceful, depicted government as restrictive, paternalistic, and necessary in this most violent of worlds. Conversely, John Locke held that humankind was innately good; he therefore envisioned government simply as a guarantee of orderly and purposeful relations between persons. John Dewey, an avowed defender of the democratic process, argued that "democracy is faith in the capacities of human nature." By contrast, Konstantin Pobiedonostsev, who took a dim view of the collective wisdom of the masses, regarded democracy as loathsome. He compared any potential or actual electorate to puppets awaiting manipulation by "hidden springs."

As with modern-day liberals and conservatives, the philosophies of these authors are colored by their subjective perceptions of historical realities. What is apparent to one is denied by another. Thus, the nature of the political spectrum is such that its ultimate roots are grounded in the life experiences and values of those composing it.

"During the time men live without a common power . . . they are in that condition which is called war."

Government Is Founded To Control Human Violence

Thomas Hobbes

The philosophy of Thomas Hobbes (1588-1679) has become a cornerstone of many of the modern conservative schools of political theory. A graduate of Magdalen College, Oxford University, Hobbes held that humankind is a self-centered, highly individualistic species essentially motivated by self-interest and self-satisfaction. These attributes generate mistrust among members of the human community and place humanity in a perpetual state of war. Hobbes' famous treatise, *Leviathan*, is based upon his despairing and mechanistic view of the human condition. In it, he claims that the choice for each individual was clear: Either live in constant fear of violent death in an anarchical state of nature or yield, along with all others, to the authority of a higher force. The following viewpoint, excerpted from *Leviathan*, offers a powerful depiction of life in the state of nature and the reasons for permanently abandoning it.

As you read, consider the following questions:

1. According to Hobbes, what are the "three principal causes of quarrel" found in human nature?
2. What examples does the author offer to illustrate that people distrust each other?

Thomas Hobbes, *Leviathan*. Published in England, 1651.

In the nature of man, we find three principal causes of quarrel. First, competition; secondly, diffidence; thirdly, glory.

The first makes men invade for gain; the second, for safety; and the third, for reputation. The first use violence, to make themselves masters of other men's persons, wives, children, and cattle; and second, to defend them; the third, for trifles, as a word, a smile, a different opinion, and any other sign of undervalue, either direct in their persons, or by reflection in their kindred, their friends, their nation, their profession, or other name.

Hereby it is manifest that, during the time men live without a common power to keep them all in awe, they are in that condition which is called war; and such a war as is of every men against every man. For *war* consists not in battle only, . . . but in the known disposition thereto, during all the time there is no assurance to the contrary. All other time is *peace*.

All Are Enemies

Whatsoever therefore is consequent to a time of war, where every man is enemy to every man, the same is consequent to the time wherein men live without other security than what their own strength, and their own invention, shall furnish them withal. In such condition, there is no place for industry, because the fruit thereof is uncertain; and consequently no culture of the earth; no navigation nor use of the commodities that may be imported by sea; no commodious building; no instruments of moving, and removing, such things as require much force; no knowledge of the face of the earth; no account of time; no arts; no letters; no society and, which is the worst of all, continual fear, and danger of violent death; and the life of man, solitary, poor, nasty, brutish, and short.

Actions Speak Loudly

It may seem strange to some man that has not well weighted these things that nature should thus dissociate, and render men apt to invade and destroy one another; and he may therefore, not trusting to this inference, made from the passions, desire perhaps to have the same confirmed by experience. Let him therefore consider with himself: when taking a journey, he arms himself, and seeks to go well accompanied; when going to sleep, he locks his doors; when even in his house he locks his chests; and this when he knows there be laws, and public officers, armed, to revenge all injuries shall be done him; what opinion he has of his fellow-subjects, when he rides armed; of his fellow citizens, when he locks his doors; and of his children and servants, when he locks his chests. Does he not there as much accuse mankind by his actions as I do by my words? But neither of us accuse man's nature in it. The desire, and other passions of man, are in themselves no sin. No more are the actions that proceed from those passions, till they know a law that forbids them, which till laws be made they cannot know, nor can any law be made till they have agreed upon the person that shall make it. . . .

A Contract for All

Each contract of each particular state is but a clause in the great primeval contract of eternal society, linking the lower with the higher natures, connecting the visible and invisible world, according to a fixed compact sanctioned by the inviolable oath which holds all physical and all moral natures, each in their appointed place. This law is not subject to the will of those, who by an obligation above them, and infinitely superior, are bound to submit their will to that law. . . . But if . . . the law is broken, nature is disobeyed, and the rebellious are outlawed, cast forth, and exiled from this world of reason, and order, and peace, and virtue, and fruitful penitence, into the antagonist world of madness, discord, vice, confusion, and unavailing sorrow.

Edmund Burke, *Reflections on the Revolution in France,* 1790.

To this war of every man against every man this also is consequent: that nothing can be unjust. The notions of right and wrong, justice and injustice, have there no place. Where there is no common power, there is no law: where no law, no injustice. Force and fraud are in war the two cardinal virtues. Justice and injustice are none of the faculties neither of the body nor mind. If they were, they might be in a man that were alone in the world, as well as his senses and passions. They are qualities that relate to men in society, not in solitude. It is consequent also to the same condition that there be no propriety, no dominion, no *mine* and *thine* distinct, but only that to be every man's that he can get, and for so long as he can keep it. . . .

Self-Preservation

The final cause, end, or design of men who naturally love liberty and dominion over others, in the introduction of that restraint upon themselves in which we see them live in commonwealths, is the foresight of their own preservation and of a more contented life thereby; that is to say, of getting themselves out from that miserable condition of war which is necessarily consequent, as has been shown, to the natural passions of men, when there is no visible power to keep them in awe, and tie them by fear of punishment to the performance of their covenants and observation of the laws of nature.

For the laws of nature, as *justice, equity, modesty, mercy,* and, in sum, *doing to others, as we would be done to,* of themselves, without the terror of some power to cause them to be observed, are contrary to our natural passions that carry us to partiality, pride, revenge, and the like. And convenants, without the sword, are but words, and of no strength to secure a man at all. Therefore notwithstanding the laws of nature . . . if there be no power erected, or not great enough for our security, every man will, and may, lawfully rely on his own strength and art for caution against all other men. . . .

A Common Power

The only way to erect such a common power, as may be able to defend them from the invasion of foreigners and the injuries of one another, and thereby to secure them in such sort as that by their own industry and by the fruits of the earth they may nourish themselves and live contentedly, is to confer all their power and and strength upon one man, or upon one assembly of men, that may reduce all their wills, by plurality of voices, unto one will: which is as much as to say, to appoint one man, or assembly of men, to bear their persons, and every one to own and acknowledge himself to be author of whatsoever he that so bears their person shall act, or cause to be acted, in those things which concern the common peace and safety, and therein to submit their wills, every one to his will, and their judgments to his judgment. This is more than consent, or concord; it is a real unity of them all, in one and the same person, made by covenant of every man with every man, in such manner as if every man should say to every man, *I authorize and give up my right of governing myself, to this man, or to this assembly of men, on this condition, that thou give up the right to him, and authorize all his actions in like manner.* This done, the multitude so united in one person is called a Commonwealth. . . . This is the generation of that great *Leviathan*, or rather, to speak more reverently, of that *mortal god* to which we owe, under the *immortal God*, our peace and defence. For by this authority, given him by every particular man in the commonwealth, he has the use of so much power and strength conferred on him that by terror thereof he is enabled to form the wills of them all, to peace at home, and mutual aid against their enemies abroad. And in him consists the essence of the commonwealth; which to define it, is *one person, of whose acts a great multitude, by mutual covenants one with another, have made themselves every one the author, to the end he may use the strength and means of them all, as he shall think expedient, for their peace and common defence.*

And he that carries this person is called Sovereign, and said to have *sovereign power*; and every one besides, his subject.

"The great and chief end . . . of men's uniting into commonwealths, and putting themselves under government, is the preservation of their property."

Government Is Founded To Protect Property

John Locke

Unlike Thomas Hobbes, John Locke (1632-1704) believed in the natural goodness of humanity. An English philosopher, Locke argued that the original "state of nature" was joyful and characterized by rational behavior among people. All experienced equality, independence, and a general sense of security. What was lacking in the state of nature was the presence of a common power—a judge—with authority to settle quarrels which might arise between reasonable persons and to condemn the malfeasance of an occasional few who moved beyond the "laws of nature." It was this need for an "indifferent judge," one who could guarantee individual property rights and ensure the execution of his or her decisions, which gave rise to government. The following viewpoint is taken from Locke's *Two Treatises on Civil Government*. In it, he explains why humankind sought "sanctuary under the established laws of government."

As you read, consider the following questions:

1. According to Locke, why did people give up the absolute freedom enjoyed in the state of nature?
2. What three things does the author claim were lacking in the state of nature?

John Locke, *Two Treatises on Civil Government*. Published in England, 1690.

To understand political power aright, and derive it from its original, we must consider, what state all men are naturally in, and that is, a state of perfect freedom to order their actions, and dispose of their possessions and persons, as they think fit, within the bounds of the law of nature, without asking leave, or depending upon the will of any other man.

A state also of equality, wherein all the power and jurisdiction is reciprocal, no one having more than another; there being nothing more evident, than that creatures of the same species and rank, promiscuously born to all the same advantages of nature, and the use of the same faculties, should also be equal one amongst another without subordination or subjection. . . .

The End of Government

If man in the state of nature be so free as has been said; if he be absolute lord of his own person and possesions; equal to the greatest and subject to no body, why will he part with his freedom? Why will he give up this empire, and subject himself to the dominion and control of any other power? To which 'tis obvious to answer, that though in the state of nature he hath such a right, yet the enjoyment of it is very uncertain and constantly exposed to the invasion of others; for all being kings as much as he, every man his equal, and the greater part no strict observers of equity and justice, the enjoyment of the property he has in this state is very unsafe, very unsecure. This makes him willing to quit this condition which, however free, is full of fears and continual dangers; and 'tis not without reason that he seeks out and is willing to join in society with others who are already united, or have a mind to unite for the mutual preservation of their lives, liberties, and estates, which I call by the general name, property.

The great and chief end therefore, of men's uniting into commonwealths, and putting themselves under government, is the preservation of their property; to which in the state of nature there are many things wanting.

Three Things Lacking

First, There wants an established, settled, known law, received and allowed by common consent to be the standard of right and wrong, and the common measure to decide all controversies between them. For though the law of nature be plain and intelligible to all rational creatures, yet men, being biased by their interest, as well as ignorant for want of study of it, are not apt to allow of it as a law binding to them in the application of it to their particular cases.

Secondly, In the state of nature there wants a known and indifferent judge, with authority to determine all differences according to the established law. For everyone in that state being both judge and executioner of the law of nature, men being partial to themselves, passion and revenge is very apt to carry them too far, and with too much heat in their own cases, as well as negligence and unconcernedness, make them too remiss in other men's.

Self-Evident Truths

We hold these truths to be self-evident, that all men are created equal, that they are endowed by their Creator with certain unalienable Rights, that among these are Life, Liberty and the pursuit of Happiness.—That to secure these rights, Governments are instituted among Men, deriving their just powers from the consent of the governed,—That whenever any Form of Government becomes destructive of these ends, it is the Right of the People to alter or abolish it, and to institute new Government, laying its foundation on such principles and organizing its powers in such form, as to them shall seem most likely to effect their Safety and Happiness.

Declaration of Independence, 1776.

Thirdly, In the state of nature there often wants power to back and support the sentence when right, and to give it due execution. They who by any injustice offended, will seldom fail where they are able by force to make good their injustice. Such resistance many times makes the punishment dangerous, and frequently destructive to those who attempt it.

Rise of Governments

Thus mankind, notwithstanding all the privileges of the state of nature, being but in an ill condition while they remain in it, are quickly driven into society. Hence it comes to pass, that we seldom find any number of men live any time together in this state. The inconveniences that they are therein exposed to by the irregular and uncertain exercise of the power every man has of punishing the transgressions of others, make them take sanctuary under the established laws of government, and therein seek the preservation of their property. 'Tis this makes them so willingly give up every one his single power of punishing to be exercised by such alone as shall be appointed to it amongst them, and by such rules as the community, or those authorized by them to that purpose, shall agree on. And in this we have the original right and rise of both the legislative and executive power as well as of the governments and societies themselves.

"The species of oppression by which democratic nations are menaced is unlike anything which ever before existed in the world."

Democracy Can Be Perilous

Alexis de Tocqueville

Alexis de Tocqueville (1805-1859) was a prominent liberal French politician and author of one of the classics of political literature, *Democracy in America*. Written in 1835, the two volume study analyzed the successes and failures of America's democratic experience. De Tocqueville believed that Europe could profit from the American experiment and concluded that political democracy and social equality would eventually sweep away the aristocratic institutions of the Old World. However, the Frenchman's enchantment with democracy was not without reservation. He recognized certain dangers in unbridled democracy, principal among them being the so-called "tyranny of the majority" and "administrative despotism." In the following viewpoint, de Tocqueville explains how the very nature of human equality can lead to a severe abridgement of the freedoms democracy is supposed to perpetuate and preserve.

As you read, consider the following questions:

1. What is the so-called "immense and tutelary power" referred to by the author?
2. What is the relationship of that power to the citizens of a nation?

Alexis de Tocqueville, *Democracy in America*. Translated by Henry Reeve, London, 1840.

I think that the species of oppression by which democratic nations are menaced is unlike anything which ever before existed in the world: our contemporaries will find no prototype of it in their memories. I am trying myself to choose an expression which will accurately convey the whole of the idea I have formed of it, but in vain; the old words despotism and tryanny are inappropriate: the thing itself is new; and since I cannot name it, I must attempt to define it.

A World Apart

I seek to trace the novel features under which despotism may appear in the world. The first thing that strikes the observation is an innumerable multitude of men all equal and alike, incessantly endeavouring to procure the petty and paltry pleasures with which they glut their lives. Each of them, living apart, is as a stranger to the fate of all the rest,—his children and his private friends constitute to him the whole of mankind; as for the rest of his fellow-citizens, he is close to them, but he sees them not;—he touches them, but he feels them not; he exists but in himself and for himself alone; and if his kindred still remain to him, he may be said at any rate to have lost his country.

The Immense Power

Above this race of men stands an immense and tutelary power, which takes upon itself alone to secure their gratifications, and to watch over their fate. That power is absolute, minute, regular, provident, and mild. It would be like the authority of a parent, if, like that authority, its object was to prepare men for manhood; but it serves on the contrary to keep them in perpetual childhood: it is well content that the people should rejoice, provided they think of nothing but rejoicing. For their happiness such a government willingly labours, but it chooses to be the sole agent and the only arbiter of that happiness: it provides for their security, foresees and supplies their necessities, facilitates their pleasures, manages their principal concerns, directs their industry, regulates the descent of property, and subdivides their inheritances—what remains, but to spare them all the care of thinking and all the trouble of living?

Thus it every day renders the exercise of the free agency of man less useful and less frequent; it circumscribes the will within a narrower range, and gradually robs a man of all the uses of himself. The principle of equality has prepared men for these things: it has predisposed men to endure them, and oftentimes to look on them as benefits.

After having thus successively taken each member of the community in its powerful grasp, and fashioned them at will, the supreme power then extends its arm over the whole community. It covers the surface of society with a net-work of small complicated rules, minute and uniform, through which the most original minds and the most energetic characters cannot penetrate, to rise above the crowd. The will of man is not shattered, but softened, bent, and guided: men are seldom forced by it to act, but they are constantly restrained from acting: such a power does not destroy, but it prevents existence; it does not tyrannize, but it compresses, enervates, extinguishes, and stupefies a people, till each nation is reduced to be nothing better than a flock of timid and industrious animals, of which the government is the shepherd. . . .

Two Conflicting Passions

Our contemporaries are constantly excited by two conflicting passions; they want to be led, and they wish to remain free: as they cannot destroy either one or the other of these contrary propensities, they strive to satisfy them both at once. They devise a sole, tutelary, and all-powerful form of government, but elected by the people. They combine the principle of centralization and that of popular sovereignty; this gives them a respite: they console themselves for being in tutelage by the reflection they they have chosen their own guardians. Every man allows himself to be put in leading-strings, because he sees that it is not a person or a class of persons, but the people at large that holds the end of his chain.

Beware Perfect Democracy

Where popular authority is absolute and unrestrained, the people . . . are, themselves, in a great measure, their own instruments. . . . They are less under responsibility to one of the greatest controlling powers on earth, the sense of fame and estimation. . . . Their own approbation of their own acts has to them the appearance of a public judgment in their favour. A perfect democracy is therefore the most shameless thing in the world. As it is the most shameless, it is also the most fearless. No man apprehends in his person that he can be made subject to punishment.

Edmund Burke, *Reflections on the Revolution in France*, 1790.

By this system the people shake off their state of dependence just long enough to select their master, and then relapse into it again. A great many persons at the present day are quite contented with this sort of compromise between administrative despotism and the sovereignty of the people; and they think they have done enough for the protection of individual freedom when they have surrendered it to the power of the nation at large. This does not satisfy me: the nature of him I am to obey signifies less to me than the fact of extorted obedience.

"The ideally best form of government is that in which the sovereignty . . . is vested in the entire aggregate of the community."

Democracy Is the Best Form of Government

John Stuart Mill

John Stuart Mill (1806-1873) was a British philosopher and economist. One of the leading and most progressive liberal thinkers of the nineteenth century, he advocated such advanced political and social programs as proportional representation, the emancipation of women, and trade unionism. Mill had unbounded faith in the process of participatory democracy. He was convinced that an active interest in politics would enhance the participant's sense of political responsibility. He also held that for power to be effectively and morally wielded, it should originate from those over whom it is exercised. The following viewpoint is excerpted from his *Considerations on Representative Government*. In it, Mill states why he believes that sovereignty should reside "in the entire aggregate of the community."

As you read, consider the following questions:

1. According to the author, what two principles attest to the superiority of popular government?
2. What is the author's attitude toward Communism?

John Stuart Mill, *Considerations on Representative Government*. New York: Longmans, Green, 1875.

There is no difficulty showing that the ideally best form of government is that in which the sovereignty, or supreme controlling power in the last resort, is vested in the entire aggregate of the community, every citizen not only having a voice in the exercise of that ultimate sovereignty, but being, at least occasionally, called on to take an actual part in the government by the personal discharge of some public function, local or general. . . .

The Best Polity

The ideally best form of government, it is scarcely necessary to say, does not mean one which is practicable or eligible in all states of civilization, but the one which, in the circumstances in which it is practicable and eligible, is attended with the greatest amount of beneficial consequences, immediate and prospective. A completely popular government is the only polity which can make out any claim to this character. It is pre-eminent in both the departments between which the excellence of a political constitution is divided. It is both more favorable to present good government and promotes a better and higher form of national character than any other polity whatsoever.

Two Principles

Its superiority in reference to present well-being rests upon two principles of as universal truth and applicability as any general propositions which can be laid down respecting human affairs. The first is that the rights and interests of every or any person are only secure from being disregarded when the person interested is himself able, and habitually disposed, to stand up for them. The second is that the general prosperity attains a greater height and is more widely diffused in proportion to the amount and variety of the personal energies enlisted in promoting it.

Putting these two propositions into a shape more special to their present application: human beings are only secure from evil at the hands of others in proportion as they have the power of being, and are, self-*protecting*; and they only achieve a high degree of success in their struggle with nature in proportion as they are self-*dependent*, relying on what they themselves can do, either separately or in concert, rather than on what others do for them.

Communism

The former proposition—that each is the only safe guardian of his own rights and interests—is one of those elementary maxims of prudence which every person capable of conducting his own affairs implicitly acts upon wherever he himself is interested. Many, indeed, have a great dislike to it as a political doctrine and are fond of holding it up to obloquy as a doctrine of universal selfishness. To which we may answer that whenever it ceases to be true that mankind, as a rule, prefer themselves to others, and those nearest to them to those more remote, from that moment Communism is not only practicable but the only defensible form of society, and will, when that time arrives, be assuredly carried into effect. For my own part, not believing in universal selfishness, I have no difficulty in admitting that Communism would even now be practicable among the *élite* of mankind, and may become so among the rest. But as this opinion is anything but popular with those defenders of existing institutions who find fault with the doctrine of the general predominance of self-interest, I am inclined to think they do in reality believe that most men consider themselves before other people. It is not, however, necessary to affirm even thus much in order to support the claim of all to participate in the sovereign power. We need not suppose that when power resides in an exclusive class, that class will knowingly and deliberately sacrifice the other classes to themselves; it suffices that, in the absence of its natural defenders, the interest of the excluded is always in danger of being overlooked, and, when looked at, is seen with very different eyes from those of the persons whom it directly concerns. . . .

Citizens Must Participate

The better the constitution of a State is, the more do public affairs encroach on private in the minds of the citizens. Private affairs are even of much less importance, because the aggregate of the common happiness furnishes a greater proportion of that of each individual, so that there is less for him to seek in particular cares. In a well-ordered city every man flies to the assemblies: under a bad government no one cares to stir a step to get to them, because no one is interested in what happens there, because it is foreseen that the general will will not prevail, and lastly because domestic cries are all-absorbing. Good laws lead to the making of better ones; bad ones bring about worse. As soon as any man says of the affairs of the State *What does it matter to me?* the State may be given up for lost.

Jean Jacques Rousseau, *Social Contract*, 1762.

It is evident that the only government which can fully satisfy all the exigencies of the social state is one in which the whole people participate; they any paticipation, even in the smallest public function, is useful; that the participation should everywhere be as great as the general degree of improvement of the community will allow; and that nothing less can be ultimately desirable than the admission of all to a share in the sovereign power of the state. But since all cannot, in a community exceeding a single small town, participate personally in any but some very minor portions of the public business, it follows that the ideal type of a perfect government must be representative.

Distinguishing Between Revolution and Change

The following exercise will explore your attitude toward change. Sometimes change brings progress; other times pain and suffering. Frequently both progress and human suffering are by-products of social, political, scientific, and technological change. Change can occur slowly or it can come suddenly (revolutionary change). The attitude toward change is a major difference distinguishing liberals and conservatives.

Consider each of the following situations carefully. Mark R for situations that you believe demand revolutionary change. Mark G whenever you think gradual change is needed. Mark S if you think the status quo should be maintained (no change needed). Record the total number of Rs, Gs and Ss you mark. On the basis of these totals, decide if you tend to be liberal or conservative in terms of change.

> R = *revolutionary change*
> G = *gradual change*
> S = *status quo*

1. The Social Security System
2. Welfarism in the US
3. A comprehensive nuclear test ban treaty with the USSR
4. The rights of gays
5. A more equitable sharing of the nation's wealth
6. Equal rights for women
7. Military spending by the federal government
8. Federal guidelines on air and water pollution
9. Immigration policy
10. US policy regarding Central America

"The tendency of universal suffrage, is to jeopardize the the rights of property, and the principles of liberty."

Popular Sovereignty Is a Danger

James Kent

James Kent (1763-1847) was one of the nineteenth century's leading legal scholars and jurists. A chancellor of the courts of New York State, he also served three legislative terms in the New York assembly. He is perhaps best known for his *Commentaries on American Law*, a systematic legal treatise which greatly influenced the teaching and practice of law in the United States. Kent, a philosophical conservative, was vehemently opposed to universal suffrage. He believed instead that voting should be limited to the propertied interests of the nation. In the following viewpoint, he explains his opposition to an extension of voting privileges. Although Kent was specifically addressing himself to proposed changes in New York State's constitution, his remarks embody principles widely held by the conservative mind of his day.

As you read, consider the following questions:

1. According to the author, what group represents the lending and governing interests of his state? What qualities does he claim that group possesses?
2. Why does the author believe that universal suffrage would "jeopardize the rights of property, and the principles of liberty?"

Excerpted from *Reports of the Proceedings and Debates of the Convention of 1821.* Albany, New York, 1821.

We are engaged in the bold and hazardous experiment of remodeling the constitution. . . .

The senate has hitherto been elected by the farmers of the state—by the free and independent lords of the soil, worth at least $250 in freehold estate over and above all debts charged thereon. The governor has been chosen by the same electors, and we have hitherto elected citizens of elevated rank and character. Our assembly has been chosen by freeholders, possessing a freehold of the value of $50, or by persons renting a tenement of the yearly value of $5, and who have been rated and actually paid taxes to the state. By the report before us, we propose to annihilate, at one stroke, all those property distinctions and to bow before the idol of universal suffrage. That extreme democratic principle, when applied to the legislative and executive departments of government, has been regarded with terror, by the wise men of every age, because in every European republic, ancient and modern, in which it has been tried, it has terminated disastrously, and been productive of corruption, injustice, violence, and tyranny. And dare we flatter ourselves that we are a peculiar people, who can run the career of history, exempted from the passions which have disturbed and corrupted the rest of mankind? If we are like other races of men, with similar follies and vices, then I greatly fear that our posterity will have reason to deplore in sackcloth and ashes, the delusion of the day. . . .

The Agricultural Interests

The great leading and governing interest of this state, is, at present, the agricultural; and what madness would it be to commit that interest to the winds. The great body of the people, are now the owners and actual cultivators of the soil. With that wholesome population we always expect to find moderation, frugality, order, honesty, and a due sense of independence, liberty, and justice. It is impossible that any people can lose their liberties by internal fraud or violence, so long as the country is parcelled out among freeholders of moderate possessions, and those freeholders have a sure and efficient control in the affairs of the government. Their habits, sympathies, and employments, necessarily inspire them with a correct spirit of freedom and justice; they are the safest guardians of property and the laws. . . .

A Perceived Danger

The apprehended danger from the experiment of universal suffrage applied to the whole legislative department, is no dream of the imagination. It is too mighty an excitement for the moral constitution of men to endure. The tendency of universal suffrage, is to jeopardize the rights of property, and the principles of liberty. There is a constant tendency in human society, and the history of every age proves it; there is a tendency in the poor to covet

74

and to share the plunder of the rich; in the debtor to relax or avoid the obligation of contracts; in the majority to tyrannize over the minority, and trample down their rights; in the indolent and the profligate, to cast the whole burthens of society upon the industrious and the virtuous; and *there is a tendency in ambitious and wicked men, to inflame these combustible materials. . . .*

Unreasonable and Unjust

The notion that every man that works a day on the road, or serves an idle hour in the militia, is entitled as of right to an equal participation in the whole power of the government, is most unreasonable, and has no foundation in justice. We had better at once discard from the report such a nominal test of merit. If such persons have an equal share in one branch of the legislature, it is surely as much as they can in justice or policy demand. Society is an association for the protection of property as well as of life, and the individual who contributes only one cent to the common stock, ought not to have the same power and influnce in directing the property concerns of the partnership, as he who contributes his thousands. He will not have the same inducements to care, and diligence, and fidelity. His inducements and his temptation would be to divide the whole capital upon the principles of an agrarian law. . . .

Universal suffrage once granted, is granted forever, and never can be recalled. There is no retrograde step in the rear of democracy. However mischievous the precedent may be in its consequences, or however fatal in its effects, universal suffrage never can be recalled or checked, but by the strength of the bayonet. We stand, therefore, this moment, on the brink of fate, on the very edge of the precipice. If we let go our present hold on the senate, we commit our proudest hopes and our most precious interests to the waves.

"So far . . . as the people can with convenience speak, it is safer for them to express their own will."

Popular Sovereignty Is Necessary

Andrew Jackson

Andrew Jackson (1767-1845) was the seventh President of the United States (1829-1837). A former congressman and military hero, he advocated, throughout most of his public life, increased popular participation in government. Although Jackson was not a political philosopher per se, he was instrumental in furthering the concept of participatory democracy in the US by virtue of his high office, enormous popularity, and energetic pursuit of principles. His impact was such that historians use the term "Jacksonian Democracy" when referring to the period in which he flourished. The following viewpoint is taken from Jackson's first Annual Message to Congress delivered on December 8, 1829. In it, he offers an eloquent plea favoring the direct election of President and Vice-President of the United States.

As you read, consider the following questions:

1. What argument does the author offer supporting the selection of the President and Vice-President by direct election of the people?
2. What does the author write regarding the removal of a public official from office?

Excerpted from *A Compilation of the Messages and Papers of the Presidents, 1789-1897*, II, James D. Richardson, editor. Washington, DC: Government Printing Office, 1897.

I consider it one of the most urgent of my duties to bring to your attention the propriety of amending that part of our Constitution which relates to the election of President and Vice-President. Our system of government was by its framers deemed an experiment, and they therefore consistently provided a mode of remedying its defects.

To the people belongs the rights of electing their Chief Magistrate; it was never designed that their choice should in any case be defeated, either by the intervention of electoral colleges or by the agency confided, under certain contingencies, to the House of Representatives. Experience proves that in proportion as agents to execute the will of the people are multiplied there is danger of their wishes being frustrated. Some may be unfaithful; all are liable to err. So far, therefore, as the people can with convenience speak, it is safer for them to express their own will.

Majority Must Govern

The number of aspirants to the Presidency and the diversity of the interests which may influence their claims leave little reason to expect a choice in the first instance, and in that event the election must devolve on the House of Representatives, where it is obvious the will of the people may not be always ascertained, or, if ascertained, may not be regarded. From the mode of voting by States the choice is to be made by 24 votes, and it may often occur that one of these will be controlled by an individual Representative. Honors and offices are at the disposal of the successful candidate. Repeated ballotings may make it apparent that a single individual holds the cast in his hands. May he not be tempted to name his reward? But even without corruption, supposing the probity of the Representative to be proof against the powerful motives by which it may be assailed, the will of the people is still constantly liable to be misrepresented. One may err from ignorance of the wishes of his constituents; another from a conviction that it is his duty to be governed by his own judgment of the fitness of the candidates; finally, although all were inflexibly honest, all accurately informed of the wishes of their constituents, yet under the present mode of election a minority may often elect a President, and when this happens it may reasonably be expected that efforts will be made on the part of the majority to rectify this injurious operation of their institutions. But although no evil of this character should result from such a perversion of the first principle of our system—that the majority is to govern—it must be very certain that a President elected by a minority can not enjoy the confidence necessary to the successful discharge of his duties.

In this as in all other matters of public concern policy requires that as few impediments as possible should exist to free operation of the public will. . . .

There are, perhaps, few men who can for any great length of

77

time enjoy office and power without being more or less under the influence of feelings unfavorable to the faithful discharge of their public duties. Their integrity may be proof against improper considerations immediately addressed to themselves, but they are apt to acquire a habit of looking with indifference upon the public interests and of tolerating conduct from which an unpracticed man would revolt. Office is considered as a species of property, and government rather as a means of promoting individual interests than as an instrument created solely for the service of the people. Corruption in some and in others a perversion of correct feelings and principles divert government from its legitimate ends and make it an engine for the support of the few at the expense of the many. The duties of all public officers are, or at least admit of being made, so plain and simple that men of intelligence may readily qualify themselves for their performance; and I can not but believe that more is lost by the long continuance of men in office than is generally to be gained by their experience. I submit, therefore, to your consideration whether the efficiency of the Government would not be promoted and official industry and integrity better secured by a general extension of the law which limits appointments to four years.

A Healthy Solution

In a country where offices are created solely for the benefit of the people no one man has any more intrinsic right to official station than another. Offices were not established to give support to particular men at the public expense. No individual wrong is, therefore, done by removal, since neither appointment to nor continuance in office, is matter of right. The incumbent became an officer with a view to public benefits, and when these require his removal they are not to be sacrificed to private interests. It is the people, and they alone, who have a right to complain when a bad officer is substituted for a good one. He who is removed has the same means of obtaining a living that are enjoyed by the millions who never held office. The proposed limitations would destroy the idea of property now so generally connected with official station, and although individual distress may be sometimes produced, it would, by promoting the rotation which constitutes a leading principle in the republican creed, give healthful action to the system.

"Democracy now aspires to universal suffrage—a fatal error, and one of the most remarkable in the history of mankind."

Government by All Is Disastrous

Konstantin Pobiedonostsev

Konstantin Pobiedonostsev (1827-1907), a Russian jurist and professor of civil law at Moscow, became a prominent member of the Russian court in 1865 when he attracted the attention of Tsar Alexander II. Under his powerful influence, the Tsarist government intensified already existing reactionary policies such as censorship, suppression of opposition opinion, and persecution of unorthodox religious minorities. Pobiedonostsev's lifelong mistrust of democratic reform, especially as it related to popular participation in government, bordered on paranoia. Although his influence upon Western political thought and practice was negligible compared to others in this chapter, the principles he embraced and so fervently articulated have frequently surfaced and impacted upon the social and political life of various nations throughout much of the modern era. The following viewpoint, excerpted from his *Reflections of a Russian Statesman*, evidences Pobiedonostsev's disdain for democracy and the common people.

As you read, consider the following questions:

1. According to the author, who are the "real rulers" in a democratic state?
2. What political system, claims the author, produces the "most necessary and fruitful reforms?"

Konstantin Petrovich Pobiedonostsev, *Reflections of a Russian Statesman*, translated by R.C. Long. London: Grant Richards, 1898.

The passionate apostles of freedom mistake in assuming freedom in equality. Bitter experience has proven a hundred times that freedom does not depend from equality, and that equality is in no wise freedom. . . .

What Is Freedom?

What is this freedom by which so many minds are agitated, which inspires so many insensate actions, so many wild speeches, which leads the people so often to misfortune? In the democratic sense of the word, freedom is the right of political power, or, to express it otherwise, the right to participate in the government of the State. This universal aspiration for a share in government has no constant limitations, and seeks no definite issue, but incessantly extends. . . . Forever extending its base, the new Democracy now aspires to universal suffrage—a fatal error, and one of the most remarkable in the history of mankind. By this means, the political power so passionately demanded by Democracy would be shattered into a number of infinitesimal bits, of which each citizen acquires a single one. Each vote, representing an inconsiderable fragment of power, by itself signifies nothing. . . . He who controls a number of these fragmentary forces is master of all power. . . . In a Democracy, the real rulers are the dexterous manipulators of votes, with their placemen, the mechanics who so skilfully operate the hidden springs which move the puppets in the arena of democratic elections. Men of this kind are ever ready with loud speeches lauding equality; in reality, they rule the people as any despot or military dictator might rule it.

The extension of the right to participate in elections is regarded as progress and as the conquest of freedom by democratic theorists, who hold that the more numerous the participants in political rights, the greater is the probability that all will employ this right in the interests of the public welfare, and for the increase of the freedom of the people. Experience proves a very different thing. The history of mankind bears witness that the most necessary and fruitful reforms—the most durable measures—emanated from the supreme will of one statesman, or from a minority enlightened by lofty ideas and deep knowledge, and that, on the contrary, the extension of the representative principle is accompanied by an abasement of political ideas and the vulgarisation of opinions in the mass of the electors. Its shows also that this extension—in great States—was inspired by secret aims to the centralization of power, or led directly to dictatorship. . . .

A False Principle

Among the falsest of political principles is the principle of the sovereignty of the people, the principle that all power issues from the people, and is based upon the national will—a principle which has unhappily become more firmly established since the time of the French Revolution. Thence proceeds the theory of Parliamentarism. . . . In what does the theory of Parliamentarism consist?

Perish with Democracy

I have not the slightest doubt that, if we had a purely democratic government here, the effect would be the same. Either the poor would plunder the rich, and civilization would perish, or order and property would be saved by a strong military government, and liberty would perish.

Thomas Macaulay, Letter to Henry S. Randall, May 23, 1857.

It is supposed that the people in its assemblies makes its own laws, and elects responsible officers to execute its will. . . . [But] on the day of polling few give their votes intelligently; these are the individuals, influential electors whom it has been worth while to convince in private. The mass of electors, after the practice of the herd, votes for one of the candidates nominated by the committees. Not one exactly knows the man, or considers his character, his capacity, his convictions; all vote merely because they have heard his name so often. It would be vain to struggle against this herd. . . .

Unworthy Individuals

In theory, the election favors the intelligent and capable; in reality, it favors the pushing and impudent. It might be thought that education, experience, conscientiousness in work, and wisdom in affairs, would be essential requirements in the candidate; in reality, whether these qualities exist or not, they are in no way needed in the struggle of the election, where the essential qualities are audacity, a combination of impudence and oratory, and even some vulgarity, which invariably acts on the masses; modesty, in union with delicacy of feeling and thought, is worth nothing.

"What the argument for democracy implies is that the best way to produce initiative and constructive power is to exercise it."

Government by All Is Wisest

John Dewey

John Dewey (1859-1952) was one of America's leading philosophers. His ideas on education, social psychology, and political philosophy effected several generations of intellectual thought in America and the world. The author of *Democracy and Education* (1916) and *Liberalism and Social Action* (1935), Dewey viewed democracy as a primary ethical value, the absence or severe restriction of which could greatly diminish the political, social, and moral health of a nation. His democratic ideals profoundly influenced the so-called Progressive School of education. The following viewpoint offers Dewey's views of the form and substance of democracy. Excerpted from an address delivered to the National Education Association, it is one of the most enthusiastic and compelling endorsements of democracy presented by a prominent American.

As you read, consider the following questions:

1. According to the author, the foundation of democracy is founded upon what belief? Upon what belief rests autocratic and authoritarian actions?
2. Does the author believe that all people are equal in natural endowments? Explain your answer.

John Dewey, "Democracy and Educational Education," *School and Society*, 45, April 3, 1937. From an address presented before the National Educational Association, February 22, 1937.

Democratic political forms are simply the best means that human wit has devised up to a special time in history. But they rest back upon the idea that no man or limited set of men is wise enough or good enough to rule others without their consent; the positive meaning of this statement is that all those who are affected by social institutions must have a share in producing and managing them. . . .

Foundation of Democracy

The foundation of democracy is faith in the capacities of human nature; faith in human intelligence and in the power of pooled and cooperative experience. It is not belief that these things are complete but that if given a show they will grow and be able to generate progressively the knowledge and wisdom needed to guide collective action. Every autocratic and authoritarian scheme of social action rests on a belief that the needed intelligence is confined to a superior few, who because of inherent natural gifts are endowed with the ability and the right to control the conduct of others; laying down principles and rules and directing the ways in which they are carried out. . . .

Equality of Opportunity

Belief in equality is an element of the democratic credo. It is not, however, belief in equality of natural endowments. Those who proclaimed the idea of equality did not suppose they were enunciating a psychological doctrine, but a legal and political one. All individuals are entitled to equality of treatment by law and in its administration. Each one is affected equally in quality if not in quantity by the institutions under which he lives and has an equal right to express his judgment, although the weight of his judgment may not be equal in amount when it enters into the pooled result to that of others. In short, each one is equally an individual and entitled to equal opportunity of development of his own capacities, be they large or small in range. Moreover, each has needs of his own, as significant to him as those of others are to them. The very fact of natural and psychological inequality is all the more reason for establishment by law of equality of opportunity, since otherwise the former becomes a means of oppression of the less gifted.

Let All Contribute

While what we call intelligence be distributed in unequal amounts, it is the democratic faith that it is sufficiently general so that each individual has something to contribute, whose value can be assessed only as enters into the final pooled intelligence constituted by the contributions of all. Every authoritarian scheme, on the contrary, assumes that its value may be assessed by some *prior* principle, if not of family and birth or race and color or possession of material wealth, then by the position and rank a person occupies in the existing social scheme. The democratic faith in equality is the faith that each individual shall have the chance and opportunity to contribute whatever he is capable of contributing and that the value of his contribution be decided by its place and function in the organized total of similar contributions, not on the basis of prior status of any kind whatever. . . .

Danger of Apathy

Absence of participation tends to produce lack of interest and concern on the part of those shut out. The result is a corresponding lack of effective responsiblity. Automatically and unconsciously, if not consciously, the feeling develops, "This is none of our affair; it is the business of those at the top; let that particular set of Georges do what needs to be done." The countries in which autocratic government prevails are just those in which there is least public spirit and the greatest indifference to matters of general as distinct from personal concern.

. . .Where there is little power, there is correspondingly little sense of positive responsibility. It is enough to do what one is told to do sufficiently well to escape flagrant unfavorable notice. About larger matters, a spirit of passivity is engendered. In some cases, indifference passes into evasion of duties when not directly under the eye of a supervisor; in other cases, a carping, rebellious spirit is engendered. . . . habitual exclusion has the effect of reducing a sense of responsibility for what is done and its consequences. What the argument for democracy implies is that the best way to produce initiative and constructive power is to exercise it. Power, as well as interest, comes by use and practice. . . . It is also true that incapacity to assume the responsibilities involved in having a voice in shaping policies is bred and increased by conditions in which that responsibility is denied.

Discerning Liberal and Conservative Stances

The Eight Major Principles of the Liberal/Conservative Debate

Liberalism	*Conservatism*
1. Regulated and planned economy	Free-market economy
2. Redistribution	Property rights
3. Welfare state	Minimal state
4. Experimentalism	Traditionalism
5. Due Process	Law and order
6. Democratism	Republicanism
7. Federalism	States' rights
8. International globalism	Nationalistic anti-communism

Examine above the eight major principles of the liberal/conservative debate. Next, look at the current issues listed on the next page. Using the information and opinions you have studied in the first two chapters of this book, relate each of the current issues to a specific principle of contention that separates liberals and conservatives in the diagram above. Predict what position each *ism* would take on the following current issues, based on the principles each *ism* supports.

Current Issues

1. Current American immigration policy
2. US relations with South Africa
3. US relations with Nicaragua
4. Federal handgun controls
5. A constitutional amendment to prohibit abortion
6. Use of the death penalty for violent criminals
7. Welfare payments to unmarried mothers of multiple children
8. A military draft of all young American males
9. A military draft of all young American males and females
10. Strict laws to protect the environment

The eight-principle comparison used above is taken from Peter Navarro's book, *The Policy Game*, New York: John Wiley & Sons, 1984.

Bibliography

The following list of books includes the works of prominent modern conservative and liberal political theorists.

Mikhail A. Bakunin

Political Philosophy of Bakunin, G.P. Maximoff, ed. New York: Free Press, 1964.

Jeremy Bentham

Introduction to the Principles of Morals and Legislation. New York: Methuen, 1982.

Thomas Carlyle

On Heroes, Carl Niemeyer, ed. Lincoln, NE: University of Nebraska Press, 1966.

Joseph M. de Maistre

Essay on the Generative Principle of Political Constitutions. Delmar, NY: Scholastic Facsimiles, 1977.

Milton Friedman

Capitalism and Freedom. Chicago: University of Chicago Press, 1981.

George Wilhelm Friedrich Hegel

Lectures on the Philosophy of History, J. Sibree, trans. London: G. Bell and Sons, 1890.

Immanual Kant

Kant's Political Writings, H. Reiss, ed. New York: Cambridge University Press, 1970.

Karl Marx

Capital: A Critique of Political Economy, Vol. 1, Ben Fowkes, trans. New York: Random House, 1977.

Baron de Montesquieu

The Spirit of the Laws. New York: Free Press, 1969.

Reinhold Niebuhr

The Children of Light and the Children of Darkness. New York: Macmillan, 1977.

Friedrich Nietzsche

Basic Writings of Nietzsche, Walter Kaufmann, ed. and trans. New York: Modern Library, 1968.

Thomas Paine

The Rights of Man. New York: Penguin Books, 1984.

Jean-Jacques Rousseau

Social Contract, Maurice Cranston, trans. New York: Penguin Books, 1968.

Herbert Spencer

The Man Versus the State. Indianapolis: Liberty Fund, 1982.

Norman Thomas

The Test of Freedom. Westport, CT: Greenwood Press, 1974.

3 ^{CHAPTER}

What Is
American Liberalism?

Chapter Preface

A new political animal populates the countryside. Difficult to find because of its shy nature and small numbers, it is called the neoliberal. In the last viewpoint of this chapter, Charles Peters, himself a neoliberal, describes its habits and habitat. In the six viewpoints preceeding it, the merits of traditional liberalism are examined and debated.

In researching this book, the editor discovered that books and articles on liberalism are not currently as plentiful as they are on conservatism. If one were to flip through the pages of the *Reader's Guide to Periodical Literature* during the 1950s or 1960s, she or he would find numerous citations on liberalism. Not so today. With a conservative in the White House and the humiliating defeat of liberal Walter Mondale still a fresh memory, liberals are maintaining a low profile. Is this a permanent phenomenon or only a cyclic occurrence? Are liberals an endangered species? The seven viewpoints that follow should help the reader decide.

*"The liberal approach must be experimental
. . . .believing that no particular manifestation
of our basic social institutions is sacrosanct or
immutable."*

The Enduring Principles of Liberalism

Hubert H. Humphrey

Hubert Humphrey was affectionately called "the Happy Warrior of American Liberalism" by friend and foe. As a longtime senator from Minnesota and as Vice President in the Johnson Administration, he was responsible for much liberal legislation on agriculture, health, and social welfare. A founder of Americans for Democratic Action in 1947, his most noteworthy liberal contribution may have been his instrumental involvement in the passage of the 1964 Civil Rights Act. In addition to being an able practitioner of liberalism, he was one of its most articulate and active advocates until his death in 1978. In the following viewpoint, Mr. Humphrey presents a philosophical foundation for liberalism and a historical overview of its development.

As you read, consider the following questions:

1. How did the Enlightenment help solidify the philosophy of liberalism? What liberal principles did it help define?
2. What impact did the Industrial Revolution have on liberalism?
3. What is the welfare state, and why do liberals identify so strongly with it?

Hubert H. Humphrey, "Liberalism." Reprinted from THE AMERICAN SCHOLAR, Volume 24, Number 4, Autumn, 1955. Copyright © 1955 by the United Chapters of Phi Beta Kappa. By permission of the publishers.

Liberalism, as a political philosophy, is based on the assumption that freedom is essential for the full development of the human personality and that, therefore, men should be free. The ancestry of liberalism may be traced back to the beginnings of literate man, but its name and formal identity did not become current until early in the nineteenth century, when it was adopted as a party label in Spain and by a British reformist bloc of radicals and Whigs.

The roots of liberalism are religious, philosophical and scientific. The doctrine represents the culmination of a development which goes back at least to the words of the Hebrew prophets, the teachings of the Greek philosophers, and the ethics of the Sermon on the Mount. . . .

Liberalism and the Enlightenment

Since liberalism as a coherent and defined philosophy was a product of a series of great economic, social, and intellectual changes which culminated in the eighteenth century, it even today bears the stamp of the Enlightenment. The period of the Enlightenment was characterized throughout Europe and America by a more or less unified set of principles, attitudes and beliefs. It was a period of optimism and revolution, of naive faith and debunking. It was, above all, a period of emancipation in religion, politics, economics and art. The unifying concept of the Enlightenment was the belief in natural law. The discoveries of Newton had been interpreted as proof that there was a natural order of things in the universe, that the laws of this order might be discovered by human reason, and that these laws furnished absolute and immutable standards for the conduct of governments and men. The implications of this doctrine were many.

First, it suggested that the potentialities of human reason were limitless. If reason could discover the laws of God and nature, there was nothing it might not do. Man could reform himself, his society and his government. And if he could accomplish all this, was he not good and, even more important, was he not perfectible? The optimism of the century was based on this view of man's relationship to society and the universe. Problems were to be solved by an application of reason, and defects of character were to be removed by education. Men of the Enlightenment could, to a certain extent, agree with Condorcet that at last reason had burst into history and progress was inevitable. The Enlightenment's linear concept of progress saw all history as a process of progressive emancipation from superstition and restraints. Not only the mind of man, but history as well, was a blank tablet on which each generation could write its own record.

Second, the concept of natural law as applied to the political scene became the doctrine of innate natural rights inherent in each individual. This concept of natural rights has been persistent in the history of Western civilization. It was expounded by both the Cynics and Stoics in the ancient world, systematized and expanded by St. Thomas Aquinas for the medieval church, and formed the basis of the eighteenth-century struggle for political freedom. In this latter period the doctrines of natural rights and individualism were joined to produce the belief that all men had the right to possess that which they acquired by their own labor, to speak and write as they chose, to petition and to form combinations, and to worship according to their consciences. There is no clearer embodiment of these principles than the Declaration of Independence and the American Bill of Rights; and there was no clearer exponent of these principles than Thomas Jefferson.

The Genuine Liberal

Ideologically, the genuine liberal is familiar with Marx and Engels, as he is with all the principal ideas about human organization. But his ideological and historical kinship is not with Marx but with men like Mill, Milton, Jefferson, Oliver Wendell Holmes, and William James. He believes in the perfectibility of man. He sets no limits to the possibilities of betterment of the human condition because he sets no limits to the potentialities of the human mind. He does not blind himself to the existence of evil, but he never loses faith in the essential goodness of man.

Norman Cousins, *Saturday Review*, September 22, 1962.

Third, in economics the doctrine of natural law again combined with individualism to become the basis of eighteenth-century laissez-faire. The economists, beginning with Adam Smith, maintained that there were certain simple, universal laws governing the economic realm, which if left to function undisturbed would bring order out of chaos and general welfare out of private interests. The content of these laws was not only known by their exponents, but was pressed upon the populace with a rare, religious vigor. These simple, immutable laws were as follows: (a) All men were born with the natural propensity to trade and barter; (b) human actions were dominated by the profit motive; (c) the profit motive stimulated maximum productivity; and (d) maximum productivity was the greatest social good. Therefore, the pursuit by each individual of his own self-interest, or profit, resulted inevitably in the greatest degree of social welfare. . . .

The Impact of Industrialism

Liberalism had barely begun to express itself as a formal political philosophy when it ran into the impact of industrialism. It grew out of an essentially pre-industrial, commercial environment and yet almost immediately had to cope with the economic, social and intellectual consequences of the Industrial Revolution. The rise of huge concentrations of wealth which dwarfed the individual rendered obsolete the society of small enterprisers which Adam Smith and Jefferson had in mind. The human values of liberalism were threatened by industrialism; and the political and economic noninterventionist doctrines of liberalism made it difficult for liberals to act to protect those values. . . .

The logic of such an economic creed implicitly supported the institution of private property. Private property, however, accompanied by the onward rush of industrialism, led to the development and triumph of free capitalism and the institution of the factory and its accompanying evils. The development of absentee ownership, which stemmed from private property, further accelerated the difficulties faced by a liberalism geared to a commercial small-entrepreneur economy. With the state abdicating many important areas of activity, private interests readily stepped in to fill the vacuum. . . .

Twentieth-century liberalism thus tried to adjust itself to the realities of an industrial civilization. It met with both partial success and tragic failure. The failure was in Europe. Only in England under a brilliant Lloyd George government before World War I was a belated effort made to catch up with industrial realities. In France, the Radical Socialist party (Liberal) participated in the Popular Front of the 1930s, but even here the efforts were too late and the forces of economic power too great. Instead of liberalism, socialism, communism and facism seemed to represent a more specific response to the industrial challenge and therefore swept the working populations and the middle classes.

In the United States, liberalism did seem to make the turn and remains today a dominant political force. An expanding frontier and the blessings of natural resources were partly responsible. They provided greater freedom for action, delayed the rise of the trade union movement, and, in turn, severely handicapped efforts of Marxism to gain a foothold here. Partly responsible too were a series of brilliant political leaders who helped reshape liberalism into an instrument for dealing with industrial society. They included Theodore Roosevelt, who first saw the democratic possibilities in big government and the need for big government to meet big business; Woodrow Wilson; and Franklin D. Roosevelt, who completed the transformation of American liberalism from an antistatist creed to a philosophy willing to use the state to achieve freedom—an end shared with traditional liberalism. . . .

The Use of State Power

Liberalism today stands generally committed to the qualified use of state power to achieve the values of freedom and human dignity. Like their ancestors, modern liberals recognize that concentration of power, whether in private or public hands, is the enemy of freedom.

In the economic realm, this has led the mainstream of American liberalism in the direction of a form of "mixed economy" which would include within it a diversification of ownership. Government power would be exercised through the indirect controls of fiscal and budgetary policy, rather than through direct physical control and central committee planning. This has been accompanied politically by an emphasis on the preservation of "rights," particularly as they relate to the need for dissent and opposition within a democratic society. . . .

In thus invoking the agency of government to protect and assist the individual, liberals call attention to two profoundly important changes which government itself has undergone since the day when Gournay, the eighteenth-century Physiocrat, proclaimed the ideal of laissez-faire.

First, despite the notorious shortcomings of bureaucracy, the techniques of public administration are incomparably superior to the pre-scientific methods of the eighteenth and nineteenth centuries.

Second, and foremost, the government agency invoked by liberals is one democratically controlled and subject to the will of people who speak, write and assemble freely and who are effectively organized into political parties, trade unions, business and professional groups, fraternities, religious and other independent associations.

The Core of Liberalism

Liberalism is the credo of those who have no fear of the idea of change. Its core, as I see it, is a willingness to place human rights first and property rights second, or as Lincoln put it: "I am for both man and the dollar, but in case of conflict I am for the man."

Henry Wallace, *The New York Times Magazine*, April 18, 1948.

Accordingly, liberals have evolved a program of government action which, by a striking consensus of both critics and adherents, has come to be known as the "welfare state."

The Welfare State

The welfare state is based, in the first place, upon acceptance of collective responsibility for providing all individuals with equality of opportunity. This implies, as a minimum, the elimination of disparities brought about through racial and religious discrimination, and the universal availability of adequate educational facilities.

Second, in a society as richly endowed as our own, the welfare state assumes responsibility for the basic economic security of those who are unable, through no fault of their own, to provide such security for themselves. This implies aid to those who are disabled by reason of accident, illness, youth or old age; minimum wage legislation and unemployment insurance for all workers; and aid to economically disadvantaged groups through support of labor unions, consumer organizations, small farmers and independent business.

Third, the welfare state assumes the responsibility for reducing great disparities in the distribution of wealth and bringing about a closer coincidence between the income of the individual and his contribution to society. This implies an appropriate tax policy and a forthright attack upon monopoly and other business arrangements which exaggerate differences in income.

Finally, the welfare state assumes the responsibility for promoting the full employment of our manpower and the full utilization of our resources. These, in turn, spell the objective of full production within the limits of an intelligent human and natural resources conservation and utilization program. Thus, contrary to the contention of its critics, the welfare state is concerned with the production of wealth as well as with the spending and distribution of wealth.

One other modern challenge to traditional liberalism is represented by Sigmund Freud and the development of psychoanalysis. As man began to learn more about himself, some of the earlier conceptions of liberalism came into sharp question. The liberal faith had been based on the judgment of man as a reasonable and good being. By acquiring knowledge and applying the scientific method, man could discover the laws of the universe as they related to his problems and solve them. The end result would be good, since man was good.

The Importance of Morality

Man's study of his own psyche, however, raised disturbing doubts about these presuppositions of liberalism. Even with education, men were not necessarily guided by reason; and psychoanalysis discovered that evil was perhaps as essential an ingredient of man as good. In the latter sense, the psychoanalytic challenge to liberalism came close to the Christian theological notion of "original sin," which has had its modern political expression in the works of Reinhold Niebuhr. Since men could be "children of light" and "children of darkness" and since man's subconscious was a cauldron of complexes and neuroses which interfered with the supremacy of reason over emotion, the liberal's faith in man's reason, man's goodness, and the scientific method was severely undermined. The Nazi eruption was the cold historical symbol of man's capacity for evil.

How liberalism responds to this challenge will in large measure determine its propensities for survival. The new discoveries need not in any way lead us to doubt that the goals of liberalism are as valid today as they always have been. The new insights into man which we have achieved now make our earlier faith appear naive, but this new understanding can give us strength and direction as it places the problems faced by liberalism into clearer focus. One essential adjustment which we must make is the need to embrace morality as an active, aggressive force in modern life. We can no longer take morality for granted and assume its superiority in man or its eventual victory over the forces of evil.

The Necessity of Change

The liberalism of today, therefore, must strive to achieve freedom for man within the context of the problems which now face him. It should have no set of fixed dogmas concerning the kind of society in which individuals most fully realize themselves. Beyond a basic commitment to the dignity and worth of the individual, the content of liberalism from age to age and from nation to nation will vary with varying conditions. Liberalism may one day challenge and another day cherish the church; in one age it may seek less government intervention in economic affairs, and in another age, more; it may at one time be hospitable to the specific interests of the business community and at another time it may be hostile. The liberal approach must be experimental, the solution tentative, the test pragmatic. Believing that no particular manifestation of our basic social institutions is sacrosanct or immutable, there should be a willingness to re-examine and reconstruct institutions in the light of new needs.

Liberalism, therefore, lacks the finality of a creed, and thus it is without the allure of those dogmas which attract the minds of men by purporting to embody final truth. Whether liberalism can survive in a world seeking security and finality cannot now be predicted. If it does not, our civilization perishes with it. Our task, therefore, is to strengthen and support it with all of our energies and intelligence. We must release ourselves from the shackles of yesterday's traditions and let our minds be bold. . . .

Finally, liberalism must cement its destiny with that of democratic self-government and the need to protect democracy against its totalitarian enemies from within and without. In the struggle for survival between democracy and totalitarianism, liberalism finds its own struggle for life intimately interwoven. Liberalism, therefore, even as it recognizes the necessity to preserve the spirit and fact of dissent in the political community, must recognize its ultimate loyalty to a majority-rule society and to the protection of all the factors which make such a society possible.

"What we really ought to ask the liberal . . . is this: In what kind of society would he be a conservative?

Liberal Ideals
Are Only Fantasies

Joseph Sobran

Joseph Sobran is a conservative syndicated columnist who began his career in the pages of William Buckley's *National Review*. The viewpoint that follows is taken from a long essay that appeared in that conservative magazine. In it, Mr. Sobran methodically builds a case for conservatism, while at the same time attacking liberalism. In his essay, Mr. Sobran chastizes liberals for championing impossible causes when they should be appreciating the positive achievements of US society with their more sensible and practical conservative fellow Americans.

As you read, consider the following questions:

1. What point does the author make in claiming that a citizen's apparent apathy may really be a healthy contentment?
2. Why is he skeptical of the "ideal" state?
3. How does he distinguish between the terms "authoritarian" and "totalitarian"? Why does he accuse the liberal of operating on totalitarian premises?

Joseph Sobran, "Pensees: Notes for the Reactionary of Tomorrow," *National Review*, December 31, 1985. Copyright © 1985 National Review, Inc., 150 East 35th Street, New York, NY 10016. Reprinted with permission.

Samuel Johnson says:

How small, of all that human hearts endure, That part which laws or kings can cause or cure!

But the same is true of all that human hearts enjoy. Laws and kings can't produce our happiest hours, though in our time they do more to prevent them than formerly.

"To be happy at home," Johnson also remarks, "is the end of all human endeavor." That is a good starting-point for politics, just because it is outside politics. I often get the feeling that what is wrong with political discussion in general is that it is dominated by narrow malcontents who take their bearings not from images of health and happiness but from statistical suffering. They always seem to want to "eliminate" something—poverty, racism, war— instead of settling for fostering other sorts of things it is beyond their power actually to produce.

Man doesn't really create anything. We don't sit godlike above the world, omniscient and omnipotent.

We find ourselves created, placed somehow in the midst of things that were here before us, related to them in particular ways. If we can't delight in our situation, we are off on the wrong foot.

Conservatives Savor the Present
While Liberals Fantasize About an Ideal Future

More and more I find myself thinking that a conservative is someone who regards this world with a basic affection, and wants to appreciate it as it is before he goes on to the always necessary work of making some rearrangements. Richard Weaver says we have no right to reform the world unless we cherish some aspects of it; and that is the attitude of many of the best conservative thinkers. Burke says that a constitution ought to be the subject of enjoyment rather than altercation. (I wish the American Civil Liberties Union would take his word to heart.)

I find a certain music in conservative writing that I never find in that of liberals. Michael Oakeshott speaks of "affection," "attachment," "familiarity," "happiness"; and my point is not the inane one that these are very nice things, but that Oakeshott thinks of them as considerations pertinent to political thinking. He knows what normal life is, what normal activities are, and his first thought is that politics should not disturb them.

Chesterton (who hated the conservatism of his own day) has good remarks in this vein. "It is futile to discuss reform," he says, "without reference to form." He complains of "the modern and morbid habit of always sacrificing the normal to the abnormal," and he criticizes socialism on the ground that "it is rather shocking that we have to treat a normal nation as something exceptional, like a house on fire or a shipwreck."

"He who is unaware of his ignorance," writes Richard Whate-

Bill DeOre, *The Daily Morning News*, reprinted with permission.

ly, "will only be misled by his knowledge." And that is the trouble with the liberal, the socialist, the Communist, and a dozen other species of political cranks who have achieved respectability in our time: they disregard so much of what is constant and latent in life. They fail to notice; they fail to appreciate.

We can paraphrase Chesterton's remark about reforming without reference to form by saying it is futile to criticize without first appreciating. The conservative is bewildered by the comprehensive dissatisfaction of people who are always headlong about "reform" (as they conceive it) or are even eager to "build a new society." What, exactly, is wrong with society as it is already? This isn't just a defiant rhetorical question; it needs an answer. We don't have the power to change everything, and it may not be such a bright idea to try; there are plenty of things that deserve the effort (and it *is* an effort) of preserving, and the undistinguishing mania for "change" doesn't do them justice—isn't even *concerned* with doing them justice. What we really ought to ask the liberal, before we even begin addressing his agenda, is this: In what kind of society would he be a conservative?

For some reason, we have allowed the malcontent to assume moral prestige. We praise as "ideals" what are nothing more than fantasies—a world of perpetual peace, brotherhood, justice, or any other will-o'-the-wisp that has lured men toward the Gulag.

Detecting Malcontents

The malcontent can be spotted in his little habits of speech: He calls language and nationality "barriers" when the conservative, more appreciatively, recognizes them as cohesives that make social life possible. He damns as "apathy" an ordinary indifference to politics that may really be a healthy contentment. He praises as "compassion" what the conservative earthily sees as a program of collectivization. He may even assert as "rights" what tradition has regarded as wrongs.

"We must build out of existing materials," says Burke. Oakeshott laments that "the politics of repair" has been supplanted by "the politics of destruction and creation." It is typical of malcontent (or "utopian") politics to destroy what it has failed to appreciate while falsely promising to create. Communism, the ideal type of this style of politics, has destroyed the cultural life of Russia, which flourished even under the czars. The energies of radical regimes are pretty much consumed in stifling the energies of their subjects; they try to impose their fantasies by force and terror, and their real achievement is to be found not in their population centers but at their borders, which are armed to kill anyone who tries to flee. Communism can claim the distinction of driving people by the millions to want to escape the homeland of all their ancestors.

Nothing is easier than to imagine some notionally "ideal" state.

100

But we give too much credit to this debased kind of imagination, which is so ruthless when it takes itself seriously. To appreciate, on the other hand, is to imagine the real, to discover use, value, beauty, order, purpose in what already exists; and this is the kind of imagination most appropriate to creatures, who shouldn't confuse themselves with the Creator. . . .

The Wisdom and Practicality of Conserving Traditions

There is no question of "resisting change." The only question is what can and should be salvaged from "devouring time." Conservation is a labor, not indolence, and it takes discrimination to identify and save a few strands of tradition in the incessant flow of mutability.

In fact conservation is so hard that it could never be achieved by sheer conscious effort. Most of it has to be done by habit, as when we speak in such a way as to make ourselves understood by others without their having to consult a dictionary, and thereby give a little permanence to the kind of tradition that is a language.

Habits of conservation depend heavily on our affection for the way of life we are born to, which always includes far more than we can ever be simultaneously conscious of at a given moment. We speak our language and observe our laws by habit. It would be too much of a strain to have to learn a new language or a new set of laws every day. Habit allows a multitude of things to remain implicit; it lets us deal with ordinary situations without fully understanding them. It allows us to trust our milieu.

Only a madman, one might think, would dare to speak of changing the entire milieu—"building a new society"—or even to speak as if such a thing were possible. And yet this is the current political idiom. It is seriously out of touch with a set of traditions whose good effects it takes too much for granted; it fails to appreciate them, as it fails to appreciate the human situation.

A political and legal system has to be based on the moral habits of its citizens, if it is concerned with anything more than power. To say that "that government is best which governs least" is not to yearn for anarchy: it is to say that those laws are best that don't require a huge apparatus of surveillance and enforcement. The foolishness of Prohibition was that it pitted the law against deep-rooted ways of life. Socialism makes the same mistake on an even larger scale. As Burke puts it, "I cannot conceive how any man can have brought himself to that pitch of presumption, to consider his country as nothing but *carte blanche*, upon which he may scribble whatever he pleases."

The conservative isn't embarrassed by the particularity of his traditions; he loves it. He neither shares nor understands the liberal's passion for taking positive measures to cut the present off from the past, as by erasing traces of Christianity in the law. It is Christianity, after all, that has formed our ideas of law. To accept this fact is no more to "establish religion" than writing the laws in English is to "discriminate against" people who don't speak English. Christianity is the basis of our moral idiom. Anyone who doubts this should try to imagine imposing the U.S. Constitution on a Moslem or Hindu country. Rooting Christianity out of our political tradition is like rooting words derived from Latin out of our dictionaries. It remains embedded even when it isn't noticed. There is no real point in trying to take it out or, for that matter, to put more of it in. . . .

American Liberalism Has Become Provincial

What is most striking to the foreign observer about American liberalism today is its provincialism. In the eighteenth century, when America was still a series of colonies, American liberalism was something big, directed to great principles such as the rights of man and liberty and self-government. American liberalism today has narrow horizons, something you would expect to find in an oppressed people, concerned no longer with the rights of man, but the rights of minorities, no longer with universal ideals or principles, but with local grievances. American liberalism has become the ideology of protest: diffuse, ill-tempered, and often rather cynical.

In Europe—even in Australia—liberalism is clearly distinguishable from socialism, but American liberalism, obsessed with American "social problems," seems to have no enemies to the left, but rather to have assimilated any and every section of opinion that seeks to "change society." As what I take to be a reaction against the persecution of Communists in the McCarthy era, American liberals are curiously protective towards Communism. They also seem to recognize no danger to freedom in Soviet expansion in Africa and South America. This makes their provincialism doubly disturbing—not only has it given up the universal perspective of earlier liberalism; when it does look out into the world, it refuses to see what is there.

Maurice Cranston, *The American Spectator*, April 1985.

For the modern liberal, who is essentially a man of the Left, the immediate has apocalyptic urgency. He is an active member of the Cause-of-the-Month Club, forever prescribing drastic action to prevent the world from being blown up, overpopulated, poisoned, oppressed, or exploited. He thinks a government that maintains law and order—a big job at any time—is "doing nothing"; because to his mind a steady and quiet activity is nothing more than inactivity. Though he speaks the language of environmental preservation well enough, he never pauses to imagine the "environmental impact" of his own policies on a social ecology that is, after all, no less real because he disregards it.

In short, he is always sacrificing the normal (he is barely aware of it, or sneers at it as "bourgeois") to the abnormal. Life, to him, is a series of crises, inseparable from politics. He is too concerned about our "rights" to bother about our health—rather as if a man dying of cirrhosis were to toast the repeal of Prohibition. If he ever has moments of well-being outside of politics, he has no vocabulary in which to talk about them.

But unfortunately, his vocabulary is pretty much the current vocabulary of politics, and when conservatives try to debate on his terms, their philosophy tends to appear as the mirror-image of his ideology. A few years ago the two camps were debating over the putative distinction between "totalitarian" and "authoritarian" systems. Liberals treated this as a quibble, a distinction without a difference. The debate sounded abstract and technical, as if egregious incidents of torture were simply "human-rights violations."

Valid Distinction

The distinction was valid, all right: and in fact liberals have consistently observed it in practice themselves, by preferring the totalitarian to the authoritarian, the Soviet Union and Cuba to South Africa and Chile. But conservatives failed to make the more serious and central point that the real difference between the authoritarian and the totalitarian is the difference between the bearable and the unbearable.

The story is told by those armed borders: people are free to leave Chile, because no great number want to leave; and blacks actually migrate *into* South Africa. This is not to defend the political institutions of these nations; but it is to point out that those institutions, good or bad, won't play so overbearing a role in the lives of their subjects as to make normal people desperate.

The very existence of censorship in authoritarian systems is a sign that all is not lost. The liberal can only damn censorship in a moralistic way; it doesn't occur to him that art, literature, and journalism can only be censored when they are already being independently produced. The kind of censorship exercised by regimes intent only on preserving a monopoly at the level of politics is different in kind from Communism's attempt to commandeer all the cultural energies of a nation, and to decree what *shall* be produced. It wasn't until 1978, for example, that Handel's *Messiah* had its first public performance in the Soviet Union— and even then it was accompanied by a libretto that glossed its theme as an allegory of the proletariat's struggle for liberation.

"Men can always be blind to a thing, so long as it is big enough," says Chesterton. One of the things most men are currently blind to is the total politicization of man. This development doesn't strike the liberal as particularly sinister; if he notices it at all, he thinks of it as a good thing. After all, he is a thoroughly politicized man; and isn't all of life essentially political anyway? Isn't it up to us to decide what sort of society we are going to build, what sort of laws and morals and distribution of wealth we are going to have?

The liberal has no specific objection to totalitarianism for the simple reason that he is already operating on totalitarian premises. He may be less headlong and bloodthirsty than the Communist, but he has as little regard for the past, as little sense that there may be anything in the tradition he inherits that deserves the effort of appreciation or surpasses his understanding. He judges everything in terms of a few ready-made political categories, which are expressed in a monotonous cant of "equality," "discrimination," "freedom of expression," and the like. He never thinks of these as possibly inadequate to his situation, because he never thinks of himself as working in partnership with the past, let alone as the junior partner in the relationship. Patience and humility aren't the marks of the malcontent. He is too busy making war on poverty to think of making his peace with prosperity: if the real economy doesn't spread wealth as quickly and evenly as he would like, he blames it and tries to remake it, taking no responsibility, however, for the adverse results of his efforts.

The chief objection to liberal moralism, in fact, is that it is immoral. This is equally true of all ideologies that dispense with realities they can't include in their visions. The economy, they think, has failed; the family has failed; the church has failed; the whole world has failed. But their visions have never failed, no matter what their cost in waste of human lives and possibilities. The dream itself is sovereign; to reject it is to be guilty of refusing to aspire; to embrace it is to lay claim to a moral blank check. As Burke said of the French revolutionaries: "In the manifest failure of their abilities, they take credit for their intentions."

But the conservative knows that the dream itself is guilty. It springs from a failure to appreciate the real, and to give thanks. . . .

Conclusion

The one thing the state can never establish by decree is stability, or continuity. It can only continue it. And by the same token, the state, whose main instrument is coercion, can't arbitrarily assign value to things. People value things for their own reasons; that is what it means to be valued. And one of the main considerations in the value of things is their security and permanence, which the state can interrupt in a moment but can only guarantee over the long run. Our chief warrant for thinking a thing will last is that it, or things like it, have already lasted. In the same way that crime devalues property, the prospect of confiscation or heavy taxation devalues any wealth in view. A too-active state can reduce the value of things very quickly; but the short-term political profits of activism are irresistible to many politicians. The democratic plague of inflation—devalued money—is the most vivid example.

The rule of law essentially regularizes a pre-existing "manner of living" (Oakeshott's phrase). Harry Truman's complaint about the "do-nothing Congress" was the complaint of a boor who had little grasp of his own heritage and assumed that the state should be, as C.S. Lewis puts it, "incessantly engaged in legislation." Maintenance, I repeat, is a demanding activity, and the state that maintains a traditional order against all the forces of decay is not "doing nothing." It is doing plenty. It is doing nearly all we can or should ask.

"Throughout history . . . practically every measure generally perceived as potentially beneficial to people at large has been bitterly opposed by conservatives."

Still a Liberal and Still Proud

Thomas Ford Hoult

Thomas Ford Hoult, a former president of the Association for Humanist Sociology, is Professor of Sociology at Arizona State University. In the aftermath of Ronald Reagan's 1980 landslide victory over the liberal incumbent president, Jimmy Carter, he presented a case for liberalism's superiority over conservatism. The argument he presented in 1981 is still appropriate today. His basic claim is that throughout American history citizens have benefited from liberal programs that conservatives have consistently opposed.

As you read, consider the following questions:

1. What evidence does the author present to support his claim that conservatism "is not an honorable thing"?
2. What evidence does he present to prove that liberalism is a superior cause?
3. How does he counter the conservative charge that liberals are "spending compulsives"?

Thomas Ford Hoult, "Still a Liberal and Still Proud," *The Churchman,* June/July 1981. Reprinted with permission.

During the [1980] election period, the word liberal was seldom heard except in a negative sense. Would-be liberal candidates shied from the term, using "progressive" as a cover. And conservatives said the word with a snarl.

Even so, I am still a liberal, and proud to be one.

My proclamation is not lightly made, since it means I must duck brick-bats from the left as well as from the right. On the left, these lovely sentiments are being expressed:

"Liberal talk is empty rhetoric designed primarily to legitimize the acts of an oppressor class."

"Liberal social reform has been reduced to a program of Band-Aid remedies whose most eloquent vision is making do with the inevitable."

"The ideology of bourgeois liberalism, with its cult of individual freedom . . . is almost completely discredited today."

And from the right:

"Liberalism seems stale, less a public philosophy than an incantation, a barren orthodoxy."

". . . the hypocrisy of ritualistic liberalism . . . goes a long way toward explaining why liberalism . . . is disintegrating before our very eyes."

". . . the liberal view of the world . . . has no relation whatsoever to the grim realities."

The Dishonorable Conservative Alternative

Given such biting criticisms, you might well ask why anyone, other than a masochist, would want to be known as a liberal. The answer is this:

The major ideological alternative—if one wants to avoid extremism—is to be a conservative. And that is not an honorable thing to be if you know the record. Throughout history, and continuing to this very day, practically every measure generally perceived as potentially beneficial to people at large has been bitterly opposed by conservatives, with rare exceptions for proposals that may perhaps serve as a diversionary bone to toss to restive masses or may be twisted to be especially useful to the privileged.

Consider the incredible range and historic importance of the liberating causes that conservatives have fought with all the power at their command: public education and health care; separation of church and state; the replacement of monarchy with democratic institutions; ending slavery, serfdom, and imperialism; votes for disenfranchised groups such as renters and women; consumer protection legislation; the equal right of all, including the poor, to have control over their own bodies; progressive income taxes; gun control; prison reform; academic freedom for all points of view; participatory democracy; desegregation; Social Security; the right of workers to organize and bargain collectively; monopoly regulation; workmen's disability compensation; medicare/medicaid; food stamps and school lunch programs; minimum wage law; public works to aid the unemployed; enviromental protection regulations; abolition of the death penalty; affirmative action; the ERA; citizen review boards to control policy agencies; the League of Nations and the United Nations.

And liberals have opposed, while conservatives in general have favored: censorship; narrow behavioral standards imposed on all; police-state measures; such as no-knock entry and invasions of privacy; peacetime conscription; tax loopholes, tariff subsidies, and natural resource depletion allowances; arbitrary distribution of power and privilege; a swollen military and confrontation (rather than detente) with the USSR.

Enough! Their stance on these issues suggests that conservatives subscribe to a litany of dishonor.

This Is a Liberal Country

This is a liberal country; it seems to have forgotten it for the moment, but that is what it is. Virtually every great advance in its history—independence, the freeing of the slaves, the abolition of child labor, women's suffrage, the civil rights revolution, Social Security, public health as a governmental responsibility, the right to bargain collectively with an employer—has been a liberal accomplishment. Conservatives? They have sat on the sidelines, whining about the cost, hoping nothing would change.

Donald Kaul, *St. Paul Pioneer Press*, December 2, 1985.

But there is more! Mull over the implications of this list of well-known conservatives, late and otherwise: Anthony Comstock, J. Edgar Hoover, Joseph R. McCarthy, George Wallace, Theodore Bilbo, Richard Nixon, Spiro Agnew, G. Gordon Liddy, John Mitchell, John Erlichman, H.R. Haldeman, William Rehnquist, Frank Rizzo, Ayatollah Khomeini, Anita Bryant. And how about groups of self-proclaimed conservatives?—The KKK, the John Birch Society, the American Nazi Party, the Salem witch-hunters, the Spanish Inquisition personnel, the condemners of Socrates, the crucifiers of Jesus, the red-raiders of the 1920's, the middle-class supporters of Hitler and Franco.

Liberals Oppose Arbitrary Oppression

Not all conservatives are so evil, of course, nor are all liberals heroic. Some alleged liberals—the "corporate," "laissez-faire," "dead center" varieties—are mostly fakes who appropriate a cherished title so they can more readily establish their smelly little orthodoxies (Orwell's phrase). But all genuine liberals have this honorable idea underlying every one of their causes: they oppose arbitrary oppression, whether of body or of mind. So they favor open societies, with equal opportunity for all enhanced by the social control of major means of production and distribution; and they stress the process that Learned Hand termed "the consecration of the spirit to the pursuit of truth," an enterprise dependent on open minds, on regarding knowledge as tentative, and on subjecting truth claims to empirical test. In contrast, conservatives prefer the closed hierarchies of established institutions, and concentration camps for people's minds. As a conservative acquaintance of columnist Colman McCarthy once put it, commenting on the fact that "wishy-washy liberals" expose children to all viewpoints: "That's not how I do it. In my house, my kids don't even know that liberalism exists. I'm a conservative. I tell my kids what's true, and that's that."

Conservatives defend by describing liberals as "spending compulsives" far too ready to trust government. But the reality is that conservatives are the truly big spenders. Does the military want more? Does a large industry cry for bail-out? Do "free enterprise" manufacturers call for protection from real competition? Spend! conservatives usually respond; dip freely into the public purse to answer all such requests. But "fiscal responsibility" is called for, they say—when it comes to such things as public health, clean air, or poverty programs.

As for collaboration with government, true liberalism often entails *fighting* big government or big labor, and not just big business; it depends on which entity is the major agency of oppression at the moment. In recent years, liberals have indeed allied themselves with certain government efforts, but they have done so because they are desperate, not because of free choice. They despair because they so frequently are faced with the ugly consequences of the unbridled selfishness of powerful entrepreneurs, a selfishness that can be countered only with the superior might of government.

But this does not mean that realistic liberals are sanguine about government authority. They know that if not watched carefully, government bureaucrats—in Washington or in Moscow—can be just as exploitive as are those who run General Motors.

Given all this, it is bizarre that so many Americans now claim to be conservative. They must be ignorant, I conclude, giving them a liberal benefit of doubt. Surely they are not as vicious as their chosen label suggests.

"I resent the assumption of liberals that only they truly understand human needs and suffering."

America Is Worse for Liberalism

Ben Stein

Ben Stein is former columnist for the *Wall Street Journal* and a former member of Richard Nixon's speech-writing staff. In the following viewpoint, Stein offers a categorical series of personal complaints directed at liberals and liberalism in America. He voices his resentment for the smugness, and what he calls the "cultural imperialism which dominates liberal thought."

As you read, consider the following questions:

1. What examples of "liberal hypocrisy" does the author give?
2. Why is he critical of the liberals' stand on welfare?
3. Find two examples of what Stein considers to be the liberal "double standard."

Ben Stein, "Why Liberals Give Me a Pain in the Neck," *Human Events*, November 27, 1975. Reprinted with permission of *Human Events*.

What I don't like is the way rich liberals, who have made their money through the operations of the capitalist system and who would be miserable bureaucratic cogs in a Socialist system, are nevertheless Socialists. I suspect that a large part of their motivation is a style of asceticism which has been fashionable among the rich since the time of the Pharisees. Another motivation for the rich liberals to dislike the capitalist system is that they have already gotten theirs and they don't want to be challenged by other people coming along and getting theirs.

Liberals and Morals

I don't like the way liberals of any income group assume that they have a monopoly on morality and that the only conscionable position on issues is their position. A sanctimoniousness runs in the liberal mind which is a direct descendent of the Calvinist assuredness of moral superiority.

Liberals assume that any challenge to their position comes from impure motives, often motivations having to do with "profit and loss" instead of the "human" factors that liberals allegedly consider. I resent the assumption of liberals that only they truly understand human needs and suffering.

I especially resent the claims of white liberals that they know best about how to solve the problems of the poor and the black. There is hardly any evidence that liberal programs to help the poor and the black have done much good. The ordinary operations of the capitalist system, however, have made enormous gains economically for the poor and the black. Liberals don't seem to understand that if they take a dollar from one person and give it to another, there is rarely any benefit. If the economic system produces new dollars for everyone, everyone benefits.

Liberals who send their children to private schools while advocating busing are particularly distasteful. The liberals who plead for integration of someone else's children are particularly blind to their hypocrisy.

Liberals Have Distorted Views

I resent the notion that everything that corporations do is wrong and everything that "people" do is right. Liberals don't understand that corporations *are* people. They are the people who work for the corporation, buy its products, and own its stock. There is no mechanical person who is benefited if corporations make a good profit. Real people benefit, just as real people lose when corporations lose money.

I don't like it particularly when liberals say that more money for this or that project can come out of profits. Most people don't realize that profits are small parts of total earnings for most companies and that without the profits, people, even liberals, wouldn't invest their money.

"Hey, Dad! Why do you call yourself a liberal when you act like a conservative?"

And there is nothing wrong with big profits. It's a sign of good management and creativity, which are rewarded in the artistic sphere as they should be in the management area. And the stockholders who get the dividends for those profits are often widows and orphans and most of all, pension funds. The liberals' idea that profits all go into buying Balmain gowns is just dangerous nonsense.

I resent the influence that liberals have gotten over our educational system. Even in those schools which are other than jungles of fear, students don't learn anything. Liberal parents and teachers who have seized control of the schools teach "sensitivity" and "interpersonal relations" to children who barely know how to read and write because the basics have been so badly neglected. Students will have more in life if they know how to read and write than if they have had "peer group effectiveness" training. Children who are without financial resources are not being done any favors if they are not taught how to perform the basic skills with which to earn a living. . . .

I am annoyed at the condescending way liberals look at religion and patriotism. Both of those are forces which make a people work and sacrifice for others and are genuine altruistic forces. Yet liberals scoff at them. Liberals should try to think whether this country could have been built without a sense of mission greater than the love of government money. In fact, liberals ought to think whether or not their own feelings do not constitute a religion of sorts before they make fun of others' religious practices. They might consider whether or not they have a double standard for people who think like they do as compared to people who have different thoughts. . . .

Liberal Double Standard

The liberal attitude about welfare is also worth getting furious about. They are tender and sympathetic towards the mother of 10 illegitimate children who is being supported by the taxpayers through Aid to Families with Dependent Children. Who said that that woman should be allowed to make so many mistakes and then have the state make up her losses? The liberal doesn't care about the working poor who might want to have another child but don't because they can't pay for the child. But for the irresponsible people who live off welfare, there is endless sympathy.

That is yet another aspect of the double standard, and there are more. The liberal wants to make a state in which people who have worked hard and abided by the rules are taxed to death to pay for those who do not work at anything except reproducing themselves. The liberal wants a state in which the lower- and middle-middle classes bear the brunt of all social change, while the liberals sit back with their union pay, or university pay, or inherited pay, or money they have gotten from the system they hate, and watch the action.

Another instance of the liberal lack of concern with real compassion is their attitude about environmental issues. No one doubts that there are important environmental problems. But there are also people whose jobs depend on taking a close look at environmental issues and not running off half-cocked whenever a cockroach is threatened. Trees may have rights, but they don't have as many rights as people. . . .

Liberals' Smugness

I resent also a kind of cultural imperialism which dominates liberal thought. Liberals tend to put down any cultural force, such as television, which has not been anointed by some kind of special holy water which can only be conferred by the elites of Cambridge, Mass., and Manhattan. Rock is low-life and fascistic, but tennis elbow from playing in a court that cost $40 an hour in Manhattan is deeply "in." Televison is beneath discussing in serious terms, according to your really important liberals; but ballet and the opera, which can only be seen by the rich few and which the great mass of people find boring, are immensely significant.

I resent the liberals' belief that all American greatness began with JFK and ended with him.

I resent the liberals' idea that the average American is a savage.

I resent the constant liberal putdown of what is American and praise of what is foreign.

I resent the liberals' idea that great ideas always come from the big cities and that small towns are only suitable for summer homes, that the countryside is peopled by dolts looking to shoot every person with long hair that they see.

Distinguishing Bias from Reason

Governmental officials, political writers, and others generally carry one of the labels of the political spectrum. These individuals are so labeled because of the opinions they hold regarding government, society, and human nature. Some of these opinions are based only on feelings and others are based on facts. One of the most important critical thinking skills is the ability to distinguish between opinions based on emotions or bias and conclusions based on a rational consideration of facts.

Some of the following statements are taken from the viewpoints in this chapter and some have other origins. Consider each statement carefully. *Mark R for any statement you feel is based on reason and a rational consideration of facts. Mark B for any statement you believe is based on bias, prejudice, or emotion. Mark I for any statement you think is impossible to judge.*

If you are doing this exercise as a member of a group or class, compare your answers with those of other group or class members. Be able to defend your answers. You may discover that others will come to different conclusions than you. Listening to the reasons others present for their answers may give you valuable insights in distinguishing between bias and reason.

If you are reading this book alone, ask others if they agree with your answers. You will find this interaction very valuable.

R = a statement based upon reason
B = a statement based upon bias
I = a statement impossible to judge

1. Government is the most dangerous institution known to humanity. Throughout history it has violated human rights more than any individual or group of individuals could do.

2. Liberalism today stands generally committed to the qualified use of state power to achieve the values of freedom and human dignity.

3. The liberal has no specific objection to totalitarianism for the simple reason that he is already operating on totalitarian premises.

4. People are unequal in terms of ambition, ability, intelligence, and character.

5. Throughout history, and continuing to this very day, practically every measure generally perceived beneficial to people at large has been bitterly opposed by conservatives.

6. Church-going people are more patriotic than those who do not attend church.

7. Government should only assist the completely helpless. To help others might destroy their individual self-respect and initiative.

8. America would be much better off if it were totally rid of extremist political groups such as the American Nazi Party and the Communist Party, USA.

9. There is hardly any evidence that liberal programs to help the poor and the black have done much good. The ordinary operations of the capitalist system, however, have made enormous gains economically for the poor and the black.

10. The trend in public opinion over the past generation has been toward greater liberalism.

11. Few Americans are enthusiasts of Jerry Falwell.

12. There is growing despair among thinking liberals because there are fundamental contradictions in their ideology.

13. The liberal faith has been based on the judgment of man as a reasonable and good being.

14. On welfare, the liberal tends to think all the poor (or practically all) are deserving, the conservative that they are bums and cheats who drive around in Cadillacs.

> *"The trend in public opinion over the past generation has been toward greater liberalism."*

America Is Becoming More Liberal

Thomas Ferguson & Joel Rogers

Thomas Ferguson is Associate Professor of Government at the University of Texas, and Joel Rogers is Associate Professor of Political Science at Rutgers University. Together they write "The Political Economy" column in the liberal magazine *The Nation*. In 1986 they co-authored the book *Right Turn: The Decline of the Democrats and the Future of American Politics*. In the following viewpoint, the authors cite a number of polls and statistical evidence to support their claim that the conservative shift in public policy during the Reagan years has not been matched by a shift in public opinion. In fact, they argue, American attitudes are becoming more liberal.

As you read, consider the following questions:

1. What evidence do the authors present to support their claim that America is moving to the left and not the right?
2. How do they explain the success of the conservative Reagan administration's policies?
3. What role do they attribute to the economy in presidential elections and popularity?

Has the American public shifted to the right? In view of recent legislation and executive action it is hard to argue with the proposition that a right turn in American public policy has indeed taken place. Following some much less significant precedents established by Democratic and Republican Administrations in the 1970s, the Reagan Administration has broken sharply with many of the major policies championed by New Deal-oriented Democratic (and even Republican) Presidents from the 1930s through the mid-1960s. Its current tax-reform proposals aside, it has passed extremely regressive tax legislation. It has cut social welfare programs and has made plain its desire for far deeper cuts. It has dismantled or gutted a host of regulatory programs and abandoned the view that the federal government has a major positive role to play in guaranteeing the rights of minorities and of the victims of discrimination. More than any other Administration since the 1930s, it has moved away from the New Deal tradition of multilateral internationalism and free trade. While shifting dollars away from social programs, it has sponsored the largest sustained peacetime military buildup in U.S. history. And it has vastly increased the size of federal budget deficits, thus creating system-wide pressures for a reduction in the scope of federal activity. . . .

It is vital to know if the central claim made by revisionist Democrats and Republicans alike—that a majority of the public has reached a stable, well-formed consensus on the desirability of right, or center-right, policies—is true.

We do not believe that it is. While there is overwhelming evidence of a policy realignment, there is little direct evidence that mass public sentiment has turned against the domestic programs of the New Deal, or even the most important components of the Great Society, and little evidence of a stable shift to the right in public attitudes on military and foreign policy. On the contrary, poll after poll demonstrates that the basic structure of public opinion in the United States has remained relatively stable in recent years. To the extent that there have been changes in public opinion on particular issues, most have tended to run *against* the direction of public policy. Moreover, despite major Republican victories in 1980 and 1984, recent voting behavior and trends in partisan identification provide little evidence of an electoral realignment.

New Deal Liberalism Is Growing

American public opinion has long been best described as both ideologically conservative and programmatically liberal. That is, Americans are opposed to big government, and respond favorably to the myths and symbols of competitive capitalism in the abstract. When it comes to assessing specific government programs or the behavior of actual business enterprises, however, they support government spending in a variety of domestic areas and are profoundly suspicious of big business. Similarly, Americans are strongly anti-Communist and generally hostile to the Soviet Union, but they are wary of using force in the pursuit of U.S. foreign-policy objectives and anxious to live in peace with Russia. This basic opinion structure may appear schizophrenic, but as Walter Dean Burnham, a political scientist at the Massachusetts Institute

Liberalism Is Based on Human Needs, Not Ideology

The liberal movement is this century is identified and associated with the New Deal of the first two Roosevelt Administrations. The New Deal involved political and economic changes which were a response to urgent practical demands, rather than the fulfillment or advancement of an ideology or a doctrinaire theory of political, economic and social organization.

Roosevelt's program provided for the pooling of social risks, as in the case of Social Security, and the pooling of economic risks, as in the case of the Federal Deposit Insurance program. It included such projects as the Tennessee Valley Authority and the Hydro-electric developments in the Far West. In each case, the decision was based on practical considerations—the development and distribution of power, for example, or the related problems of navigation and flood control—rather than on an ideological demand for social ownership or collectivization.

At the same time, other projects were introduced providing for greater Government control over such things as the investment market and the wages and hours of workingmen along with efforts to protect the small independent business and the independent family-size farm.

In the immediate postwar period, the liberal influence was strong in support of international programs such as the Marshall Plan, Point IV and the United Nations and its agencies. But what of liberals and of liberalism today?

Liberals have not lost their old land-marks. Indeed, it may be that they are looking at them somewhat too longingly at a time when they are no longer an adequate guide to need or progress, but certainly the initiative in economic, social, cultural and political action still rests today with those who are generally called liberals. . . .

If conservatives have a better response to the challenges of today, now is the time for them to demonstrate it in word and in action. It is not enough to declare themselves for freedom, truth and justice, or to declare themselves, even more vaguely, for "traditional" values. Conservatives can become a positive force in American history only if they demonstrate as much confidence in the future as they claim to have in the past.

Eugene J. McCarthy, "Liberal: What He Is and Isn't," *The New York Times Magazine*, September 1, 1963. Copyright © 1963 by the New York Times Company. Reprinted by permission.

of Technology, has observed, at least on domestic issues it probably reflects voter adaptation to a political system in which the government is interventionist but nonsocialist. In any case, it has been stable for at least a generation.

Within this structure, moreover, the trend in public opinion over the past generation has been toward greater liberalism. During the 1970s, and particularly after 1973, the rate of increase in support for liberalism slowed somewhat. In addition, as we will note below, there were some exceptions to the general liberal trend. But none of this amounted to a change in the basically liberal direction of public opinion.

Domestic Issues

We begin with domestic issues. Revisionist Democrats commonly claim that voter support for their party's traditional positions on typical New Deal issues—including government management of the economy; protecting the Social Security system, the aged, and workers; and, at least since the mid-1960s, medical care—has long been in decline, and that the present weakness of the party at the national level is a long-term consequence of that fact. Typically it is argued that rising incomes in the post-New Deal era have made voters more middle class, both in the sense that the majority of Americans are living far better than their parents did (and therefore no longer support social programs) and in the sense that they no longer respond positively to FDR-style attacks on "economic royalists," made in the name of the common man.

The survey data, however, do not bear this argument out. A recent effort by the Princeton political scientist Stanley Kelley to map the "salience" (that is, the importance to voters in their choice of party or candidate) of such New Deal issues found a remarkable stability in voter attitudes in presidential elections from 1952 to 1976. In 1952, 85 percent of the voters found New Deal issues salient—that is, 85 percent of the electorate cited positions on such issues as something to like or dislike about the major parties or their candidates or both. The figure dropped to 76 percent of the electorate in 1956, and varied only slightly over the next five elections, at 74 to 77 percent of the electorate. Obviously, New Deal issues have not become less important to American voters since the late 1950s. Moreover, among those who saw a position on New Deal issues as "biasing" their choice—that is, leading them to favor a particular party or candidate—the Democrats enjoyed the support of strong majorities in every election during the 1952-1976 period. The average Democratic bias was just under 62 percent. Put otherwise, if those elections had been decided solely on those issues, Democrats would have won them all by landslides. Clearly, Democratic Party identification with traditional positions on New Deal issues was a major party strength, not a weakness.

120

The stability of such attitudes aside, it is commonly argued that the public moved sharply to the right during the late 1970s on most domestic issues, and that a groundswell of popular opposition to domestic-spending programs and government regulation of business was an important reason for Ronald Reagan's election in 1980. In fact no such groundswell occurred. To the contrary, public skepticism toward business, and support for government regulation of it, actually increased on several dimensions during the 1970s. From 1969 to 1979, for example, the share of the public thinking that there was "too much power concentrated in the hands of a few large companies for the good of the nation" increased from 61 to 79 percent; those thinking that business as a whole was making "too much profit" grew from 38 to 51 percent. Over the period 1971 to 1979 the percentage thinking that "government should put a limit on the profits companies can make" nearly doubled, rising from 33 to 60 percent.

THE ECONOMIC BASIS
OF PRESIDENTIAL POPULARITY

THE IMPACT OF THE JOBLESS RATE

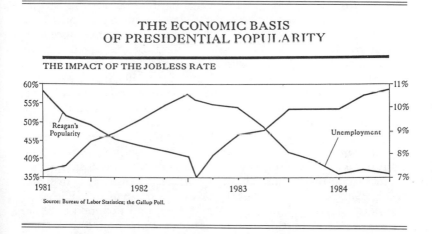

Source: Bureau of Labor Statistics; the Gallup Poll.

Nor was there any evidence of an upsurge in support for domestic-spending cuts. The National Opinion Research Center found in 1980 that only 21 percent of Americans (the average across the different spending areas) thought that "too much" was being spent on environmental, health, education, welfare, and urban-aid programs—the same percentage holding that belief in 1976, 1977, and 1978. The percentage of Americans who thought that "too little" was spent on those programs was also remarkably stable over the 1976-1980 period, dropping only from 44 to 42 percent, while the combined percentage of those who thought the amount spent was "too little" or "about right" was never lower than 72 percent. . . .

The movement in support of social-spending programs was similar. An NBC News poll found that those agreeing with the statement that Reagan was "going too far in attempting to cut back or eliminate government social programs" rose from 37 to 52 percent over 1981-1983. Comparing the results of a 1982 survey with one commissioned in 1978, the Chicago Council on Foreign Relations found a remarkable 26-percentage-point jump in those wishing to "expand" rather than "cut back" welfare and relief programs, typically the easiest target of attack among social-spending programs. Support for government action to assist the unemployed was particularly broad. By early 1983 a CBS News/*New York Times* poll found that 74 percent of the public favored a government jobs program even if it meant increasing the federal deficit. . . .

Americans Are Becoming More Liberal on Social Issues

On social issues as well, American attitudes betray no evidence of a right turn. In general, religion, feminism, civil liberties, abortion, and race relations are the policy areas in which the public has shown the sharpest increase in liberalism since the Second World War. The rate of increase has slowed during the post-1973 period, but at no time has the public actually become more conservative on these issues. And on several of the key questions highlighted by the Reagan Administration the public became more liberal over the course of Reagan's first term. Regarding abortion, for example, an NBC News exit poll in 1984 found that two thirds of the electorate endorsed the legalization of abortion, with the decision "left to the woman and her physician," while only a quarter did not. Soon after the election an ABC News poll found that the share of Americans supporting the relatively radical position that women should have a right to abortion on demand, "no matter what the reason," actually increased over Reagan's first term, rising from 40 percent in 1981 to 52 percent in 1985, while the percentage opposing abortion on demand declined from 59 to 46 percent. According to a *Los Angeles Times* poll, only 23 percent of the electorate supported a constitutional amendment prohibiting abortion, and only 32 percent of those who voted for Reagan endorsed his policy on abortion. Louis Harris reports that Americans oppose requiring school prayer by 51 to 43 percent and support passage of the Equal Rights Amendment by 60 to 34 percent. And few Americans are enthusiasts of Jerry Falwell, the most prominent leader of the religious right. A 1984 *Los Angeles Times* exit poll found that only 16 percent of the voters approved of the minister. . . .

The Reasons for Reagan's Success

But if public opinion has generally run against the right turn in public policy, why was Reagan so spectacularly popular during his first term, and especially during the first two years of that term, when most of his Administration's major programs were put in place? The answer is simple: he was not.

Press claims that Reagan's first term marked him as the most popular President of the postwar period are simply mistaken. Gallup reports that over the length of that term his approval rating—which measures satisfaction with job performance—averaged 50 percent, lower than the averages of Eisenhower (69), Kennedy (71), Johnson (52), and Nixon (56), and not far above that of Carter (47). Reagan's high point was reached shortly after taking office, when, in May of 1981, he recorded a 68 percent approval rating. Four out of the five other elected postwar Presidents had higher peaks—Eisenhower (79 percent), Kennedy (83), Johnson (80), and Carter (75)—while Nixon's 67 percent approval peak was not significantly lower. In addition, Reagan's low point of 35 percent, reached in January, 1983, was significantly lower than those of Eisenhower and Kennedy, matched the level that Johnson sank to just before he withdrew from national politics, in 1968, and came close to the 24 percent approval rating that Nixon received in July and August of 1974, just before he resigned the presidency in disgrace.

During the first two years of Reagan's presidency, when his Administration made its greatest advances, his approval ratings were particularly unimpressive. The average approval ratings for his first and second year were 54 and 44 percent, respectively. The first- and second-year average percent approval ratings for Carter (62 and 47), Nixon (61 and 57), Kennedy (75 and 72), and Eisenhower (69 and 65) were all substantially higher.

Reagan's Personal Popularity

As Reagan's approval rating fell in the polls over the 1981-1982 period, the press began emphasizing his enormous *personal* popularity. Readers and viewers were told that although the public did not like what Reagan was doing to them, they loved the man who was doing it. There is some measure of truth in this. Reagan's ratings for personal appeal have always remained well above his ratings for job performance. But press accounts commonly did not go on to point out that significant differentials between performance- and personal-approval ratings of Presidents are utterly routine, that they always show greater personal approval than perfomance approval (Americans, for whatever reason, want to believe that their Presidents are nice people), and that in fact the differential Reagan enjoyed was proportionately *smaller* than those of his postwar predecessors, not larger. . . .

Finally, it is important to stress that the policy approval Reagan did receive in the 1984 vote was almost entirely confined to judgments on recent economic performance and on hopes that the economy would continue to boom along. With economic considerations swamping other policy concerns, this led to anomalous results: vast numbers of voters cast ballots for Reagan even though they disagreed with his positions on a host of issues. . . .

The conclusion is inescapable. With the exception of the rise in support for increased military spending, which was rapidly reversed, there is little or nothing in the public-opinion data to support the claim that the American public moved to the right in the years preceding Reagan's 1980 victory. If American public opinion drifted anywhere over Reagan's first term, it was toward the left. And there is nothing in the data to support the claim that Reagan's first term marked him as the most popular President in modern times or that he has a magical hold over the electorate. . . .

The Role of the Economy in Presidential Elections

To maintain the view that Reagan's policies do not reflect a new popular consensus on policy, of course, one needs an alternative explanation of just how he has managed to win two landslide election victories. But this question has an entirely plausible answer that leads to none of the conclusions drawn by the revisionist Democrats: *the economy.*

We have already noted that Reagan's approval rating has moved in tandem with the economy, and in this he is not exceptional. A huge amount of research confirms that economic performance is an important factor in whether voters approve or disapprove of elected officials, not only in the United States but in most capitalist democracies. Indeed, quite reasonable predictions of Reagan's percentage of the two-party vote in both 1980 and 1984 can be derived from a simple model that considers only changes in real disposable income per capita shortly before an election and a measure of presidential popularity (which correlates closely with economic performance). One widely disseminated model of this type fits the 1984 case almost perfectly, predicting a Reagan percentage of 59.4 percent—only 0.2 percent off the actual result.

Such "political business cycle" models suggest that the recent problems of the Democrats are more cyclical than secular. Above all they are matters of timing. Jimmy Carter pumped up the economy in 1977 and at the beginning of 1978 but then drove it into recession just in time for the 1980 election. He thus became the first President since Herbert Hoover to run for re-election at a moment when the national income was actually shrinking, and the first elected incumbent since Hoover to lose a bid for re-election. Ronald Reagan did not make this mistake. His Administration chose to have a long and exceptionally deep recession early in its term and then (helped along by the collapse of OPEC and other factors) staged one of the greatest political business cycles in modern history, producing a 5.8 percent increase in real per capita disposable income in 1984—the largest election-year increase since 1936. . . .

That the economy was the key issue in 1980 and 1984 is also confirmed by survey data. As already noted, virtually all studies

124

of the 1980 election see it as a referendum on Carter's bad economic performance. In 1984 every major election poll found economic issues dominant in voters' minds. More immediately, and of considerable relevance to current plans to move the party to the right, a lack of confidence in the Democrats' program for the economy was the single most important reason, at the level of voting behavior, for the Democrats' defeat.

"I believe there is growing despair among thinking liberals because there are fundamental contradictions in their ideology."

The Ten Contradictions of Liberalism

Ray Shamie

Ray Shamie, a Massachusetts business leader, was the 1982 Republican senatorial candidate who ran unsuccessfully against Senator Ted Kennedy. In the following viewpoint, taken from one of contemporary conservatism's most prominent publications, *Conservative Digest*, Mr. Shamie lists liberalism's contradictions. He presents ten reasons why he thinks liberalism is in decline and will disappear from the American scene.

As you read, consider the following questions:

1. Why does the author claim liberals have not delivered on their claim to be the champions for disadvantaged minorities?
2. Why does he call liberals gullible in the arena of foreign affairs?
3. He claims contemporary liberalism will go the way of the Know-Nothing party. Do you agree?

Ray Shamie, "The Ten Contradictions of Liberalism," *Conservative Digest*, August 1985. Reprinted with the author's permission.

In recent years, liberals in Congress have come to resemble that Maytag repairman we used to see in television commercials. Remember him? He was always grousing that the washing machine didn't break down.

Like that Maytag repairman, liberals were eagerly waiting for the Reagan economy to need their repair work.

Tip O'Neill predicted during the 1982 campaign that Reaganomics would bring on another Depression.

Well, I guess it did. I've never seen liberals so depressed.

It shouldn't have surprised them, though, when the Reagan tax cuts revived the economy. The across-the-board tax cuts of the early 1960's, first proposed by John Kennedy, had the same result. The economy started growing again.

It's interesting how liberalism has changed since then.

A generation ago, it was an optimistic ideology, believing that America could change the world. Back then, liberalism called for equal opportunity, not equal result. It pushed for a strong defense, and economic growth.

It's no wonder, then, that so many liberals of that time are conservatives today.

What is *today's* liberalism? Why do we hear so much about liberals beng pessimistic, and groping for new ideas?

Is liberalism on the decline? Will it become the Edsel of ideology?

I thought it would be interesting to step back from current events as we view them on the 6 o'clock news—where issues are kept neatly separate and distinct—and instead look at an entire ideology.

I believe there is growing despair among thinking liberals because there are fundamental contradictions in their ideology. These contradictions are like cracks in a foundation, growing larger and spreading throughout.

1. It's All Relative

The first is rather abstract, but it's basic.

Liberals will often argue that everything is relative; that values like right and wrong are subjective; that there is no objective truth.

Yet they argue that only *their* theories are true.

Think about that. They say there is no objective truth, and yet if you question *their* truths, they can turn indignation into an art form.

2. Conformism

The second contradiction is the willingness of liberals to allow censorship of schoolbooks and the classics . . . and yet they want everyone to be free and do his or her own thing.

Now I'm not one to get upset if Ted Kennedy wants to refer to the founding fathers as "our founding fathers and mothers." Or as "our founding parents." But whether it's the effort to drive Huckleberry Finn out of school because it reflects the racism of that period, or whether it's the effort to rewrite history in terms of class struggle, there is in this liberalism a distinct *conformism.*

In contradiction, liberalism has propagated the idea of doing your own thing—if your "thing" is anti-the values of mainstream society.

The national head of the liberal Americans for Democratic Action is, surprisingly enough, a Massachusetts Congressman: Barney Frank. Years ago, when Mr. Frank was in the state legislature, he introduced a bill year after year to allow every community in Massachusetts to have its own "combat zone" where prostitution and pornography could flourish legally.

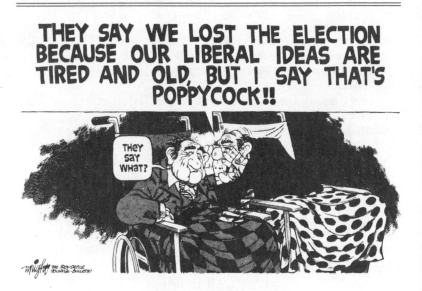

Dick Wright, Reprinted by permission of United Features Syndicate.

He was praised by other liberals for his great tolerance. I suppose you could call it an "affirmative tolerance" program.

But if there is to be tolerance of sexism in pornography, why should there be *intolerance* of sexism in the classics?

3. Church or State?

This was rarely an issue when it was mostly liberal clergy who were involved in politics. The antiwar movement and the civil rights movement would have been severely weakened if the clergy had withdrawn.

But when conservative ministers got involved in politics, this represented to the liberal mind a constitutional crisis.

When liberal clergy spoke out for liberal causes, it was an "act of conscience." But when conservative clergy spoke out for conservative causes, it was an unconscionable assault on the wall protecting the State from the Church.

4. Choice

Liberals characterize their support for funding of abortion on demand as being "pro-choice." Without getting into the arguments on abortion, the contradiction is that liberals *oppose* choice in so many other areas.

They oppose the idea of education vouchers, which would enable many poor and middle income parents to send their children to the school of their choice.

They oppose parents having the choice of sending their children to a neighborhood school, instead of being bused across town to fulfill a quota.

And so today's liberalism has a fourth contradiction: It's Pro-choice *before* a child is born, and anti-choice *after* a child is born.

5. Champions

The fifth contradiction lies in the liberal claim to be the champion for disadvantaged minorities.

The very opposite has been documented in books like *Wealth and Poverty* by George Gilder and *Losing Ground* by Charles Murray.

Welfarism has created a psychology of dependency. Instead of helping people to escape from poverty, tragically welfarism has created for millions a psychological ghetto of defeatism. The idea that society *owes* me too easily evolves into the despair that society *owns* me.

Teenage unemployment among blacks is disgraceful, yet liberals oppose legislation for a teen-wage. By establishing a minimum wage somewhat lower for teenagers, the teen-wage would give employers an incentive to hire and train young people who don't have the work experience to compete with adults.

Liberal politicians oppose such ideas becase they favor instead those welfare programs and makework jobs that keep the poor dependent . . . on liberal politicians.

6. Education

The sixth contradiction is in liberalism claiming to champion educational opportunity, while not joining the drive to restore excellence as the standard for educational achievement.

As liberals turned education into an experiment in sociology, and as an arena for politics, it's no surprise that test scores went down.

Few children, if any, will find true opportunity in life without having the basic tools of learning. As Derek Bok, the president of Harvard, put it: "If you think education is expensive, try ignorance."

7. Foreign Policy

Today's liberals will rail against American allies that are authoritarian and oppressive, and rightly so. But they consistently fail to register indignation against the larger scale oppression in the left-wing totalitarian nations.

They expressed their horror against El Salvador just two years ago. But El Salvador, as authoritarian as it was, evolved into a working democracy.

Liberals judged Nicaragua by a different standard. They were eager to recognize and legitimize the Marxist Sandinistas, yet *no* Communist government has *ever* evolved into a democracy.

It sometimes seems that the most outstanding feature of contemporary liberalism is gullibility—a willingness to accept empty words and empty gestures from dictators whose political prisons are never empty.

8. Strategic Defense

Liberals argue that they are the advocates of peace. Yet, in opposing nearly every American strategic defense program in the last fifteen years, they would have allowed the Soviet Union to achieve an overwhelming military superiority which, in turn, would have encouraged more Soviet aggression. Less peace, not more.

9. Elitism

The ninth contradiction is in liberalism preaching egalitarianism-equality for all—but believing more and more in elitism.

They used to call for "power to the people," but they don't want that. They don't want the 60% who voted for Ronald Reagan to have their way on taxes, capital punishment, busing, federal spending, and so on.

They have put their faith in the unelected Supreme Court and the unelected news media, not in the people. They have put their trust in the teachers' union, not in the parents. They have put their trust in the federal bureaucracy, not in local elected officials.

10. Future Vision

The tenth contradiction lies in the claim to represent the future, while having such a pessimistic vision of the future.

Walter Mondale said that as a [presidential] candidate he made the mistake of emphasizing too much the *sacrifice* his liberal philosophy demanded, rather than offering hope.

The truth is, contemporary liberalism is largely a program of sacrifice—where people sacrifice private economic growth for the growth of government.

These contradictions show an ideology in decline.

I believe contemporary liberalism as we've known it, will go the way of the Know-Nothing party, eventually being just a footnote in this period of American history. Perhaps historians will call them the Know-it-all party.

But there is another outlook, emerging at the same time. It begins with the four letters at the end of the word, *American*. I can.

It is the optimism of individual initiative. It begins with the imagination, not a committee . . . the imagination to dream and to aspire.

It grows with freedom, not with central planning . . . the freedom to risk and to create.

It flourishes with self-government—the only system based on the belief that there are extraordinary possibilities in ordinary people.

Because of this philosophy, our children have a tremendous future. They will explore outer space and the inner mind . . . the depths of the ocean and the depths of the human spirit.

It is a philosophy that begins, *I can*, in an America that says, *We shall*.

"Economic growth is most important now. It is essential to almost everything else we want to achieve."

The Case for Neoliberalism

Charles Peters

If Charles Peters is not the founding father of neoliberalism, he was certainly present at its creation. He is credited with coining the word neoliberalism in February 1979 at the tenth anniversary celebration of *The Washington Monthly*, the movement's most prominent publication, founded by Peters. During the 1960s, concerned with many liberals' disdain for business and the distortion of basic liberal values by impersonal and bureaucratic governmental and private organizations, he began to formulate the tenets of neoliberalism. The following viewpoint is excerpted from his frequently cited "neoliberalism manifesto" that originally appeared in *The Washington Monthly*. In it he presents the neoliberal agenda for reforming liberalism.

As you read, consider the following questions:

1. What four shortcomings of liberalism does the author claim neoliberalism will overcome?
2. Why does neoliberalism place so much emphasis on economic growth?
3. How would neoliberalism reform America's system of government?

Charles Peters, "A Neoliberal's Manifesto," *The Washington Monthly*, May 1983. Reprinted with permission from *The Washington Monthly*. Copyright by the Washington Monthly Company, 1711 Connecticut Ave. NW, Washington, DC 20009, 202-462-0128

If neoconservatives are liberals who took a critical look at liberalism and decided to become conservatives, we are liberals who took the same look and decided to retain our goals but to abandon some of our prejudices. We still believe in liberty and justice and a fair chance for all, in mercy for the afflicted and help for the down and out. But we no longer automatically favor unions and big government or oppose the military and big business. Indeed, in our search for solutions that work, we have come to distrust all automatic responses, liberal or conservative.

Perhaps nowhere have the liberal and conservative responses been more automatic than in the areas of welfare and crime. On welfare, the liberal tends to think all the poor (or practically all) are deserving, the conservative that they are bums and cheats who drive around in Cadillacs. The liberal bleeds for the criminal, blaming society for his crimes, and concocting exotic legal strategies to help him escape punishment. The conservative, on the other hand, automatically sides with police and prosecutor. Each group eagerly seizes on evidence that supports its position and studiously averts its eyes from any fact that might support the other side. . . .

Four Negative Principles of Liberalism

Behind the liberals' inability to deal with these problems were four observable if unacknowledged principles.

The first was Don't Say Anything Bad About The Good Guy. The feeling here seemed to be that any criticism of institutions they liked—the public schools, the civil service, and the unions are good examples—was only likely to strengthen the hand of their enemies. A corollary was Don't Say Anything Good About the Bad Guys, meaning the police, the military, businessmen (unless small), and religious leaders (unless black or activist). What all this meant was a shortage of self-criticism among liberals and an unwillingness to acknowledge that there just might be some merit in the other side's position.

The second principle was Pull Up The Ladder. In both the public and private sector, unions were seeking and getting wage increases that had the effect of reducing or eliminating employment opportunities for people who were trying to get a foot on the first rung of the ladder. . . .

During this time too many liberals followed the Don't Say Anything Bad About the Good Guy principle, and refused to criticize their friends in the industrial unions and the civil service who were pulling up the ladder. Thus liberalism was becoming a movement of those who had arrived, who cared more about preserving and expanding their own gains than about helping those in need. Among this kind of liberal there is powerful need to deny what they are doing, which means they become quite angry when it is exposed. . . .

The third principle is The More The Merrier. The assumption

here—and it is often correct—is that the more beneficiaries there are of a program, the more likely it is to survive. Take Social Security. The original purpose was to protect the elderly from need. But, in order to secure and maintain the widest possible support, benefits were paid to rich and poor alike. The catch, of course, is that a lot of money is wasted on people who don't need it. . . .

A New Kind of Liberalism

In recent years, some liberals who have found themselves unhappy with the conventions of their faith have begun to form a movement of renewal and reform called neoliberalism. Most press reports have described the movement as conservative, a part of a general trend toward the right.

This is wrong. We have tried to recall for American liberals the basic values concerning family, religion, community and country that they seemed to abandon to the conservatives during the 1960s and 1970s. But we continue to reject the intolerance and bigotry that has so often accompanied these values when expressed by the right.

Charles Peters, *Minneapolis Star and Tribune*, January 4, 1984.

The fourth principle is Politics Is Bad and Politicians Are Even Worse. Liberalism entered the seventies having just depoliticized the last refuge of patronage, the post office. The catch was that in destroying patronage—the last nail in the coffin was a mid-seventies Supreme Court decision that actually held it was unconstitutional to fire a political appointee for political reasons—no one noticed that democracy was the first casualty. If democracy means we are governed by people we elect and people they appoint, then it is a not insignificant fact that the people we elect can now choose less than one percent of those who serve under them. Without the lifeblood of patronage, the political parties have withered and been replaced by a politics of special interest. And since liberals assumed that patronage was always bad, they could see no answer to the problem.

Neoliberalism Stresses Economic Growth

Opposed to these four principles of the old liberalism are the primary concerns of neoliberalism: community, democracy, and prosperity.

Economic growth is most important now. It is essential to almost everything else we want to achieve. Our hero is the risk-taking entrepreneur who creates new jobs and better products. "Americans" says Bill Bradley, "have to begin to treat risk more as an opportunity and not as a threat."

We want to encourage the entrepreneur not with Reaganite

policies that simply make the rich richer, but with laws specifically and precisely designed to help attract investors and customers. For example, Gary Hart is proposing a "new capacity" stock, a class of stock issued "for the explicit purpose of investment in new plants and equipment." The stock would be exempt from capital gains tax on its first resale. This would give investors the incentive they now lack to target their investment on new plants and equipment instead of simply trading old issues, which is what most of the activity on Wall Street is about today.

We also favor freeing the entrepreneur from economic regulation that discourages desirable competition. But on the matters of health and safety, we know there must be vigorous regulation, because the same capitalism that can give us economic vitality can also sell us Pintos, maim employees, and pollute our skies and streams. . . .

Other Neoliberal Goals

Our concern about the public school system illustrates a central element of neoliberalism: It is at once pragmatic and idealistic.

Our practical concern is that public schools have to be made better, much better, if we are to compete economically with other technologically advanced countries, if we are to have more Route 128s and Silicon Valleys. Our idealistic concern is that we have to make these schools better if the American dream is to be realized. Right now there is not a fair chance for all because too many children are receiving a bad education. The urban public schools have in fact become the principal instrument of class oppression in America, keeping the lower orders in their place while the upper class sends its children to private schools.

Another way the practical and the idealistic merge in neoliberal thinking is in our attitude toward income maintenance programs like Social Security, welfare, veterans' pensions, and unemployment compensation. We want to eliminate duplication and apply a means test to these programs. They would all become one insurance program against need.

As a practical matter, the country can't afford to spend money on people who don't need it—my aunt who uses her Social Security check to go to Europe or your brother-in-law who uses his unemployment compensation to finance a trip to Florida. And as liberal idealists, we don't think the well-off should be getting money from these programs anyway—every cent we can afford should go to helping those really in need.

The pragmatic idealism of neoliberals is perhaps the clearest in our reasons for supporting a military draft.

A draft would be a less expensive way to meet our need for military manpower because we would no longer have to use high salaries to attract enlistees. It would also be the fairest way, because all classes would share equally in the burdens and risks of military service.

Those who are drafted and opposed as a matter of conscience to military service should have the option of entering a domestic or overseas peace corps. But if that option is taken, the term of service should be three years instead of two; this should help guarantee that the decision is in fact one of conscience. In the long run we hope a draft will not be needed. We want to see a rebirth of the spirit of service that motivates people to volunteer to give, without regard to financial reward, a few years of their lives to public service, including military service. But for now we realize that the fear of being a sucker, if not just plain selfishness, will keep the upper classes from volunteering.

There is another reason for our support of a draft at the present time. We want to bring people together. When I was growing up, social classes were mixed by both the public schools and the draft. Today the sons of the rich avoid the public schools and scorn the military service. This is part of a trend toward separatism—not only by race but by class and interest group—that has divided the nation and produced the politics of selfishness that has governed this country for more than a decade. . . .

Dick Wright, Reprinted by permission of United Features Syndicate.

Snobbery, like the credentialism to which it is related, is another neoliberal target. The snobbery that is most damaging to liberalism is the liberal intellectuals' contempt for religious, patriotic, and family values. Instead of scorning people who value family, country, and religion, neoliberals believe in reaching out to them to make clear that our programs are rooted in the same values.

Take school prayer. While I easily can see how the custom of my youth, requiring children to recite the Lord's Prayer at the beginning of school, was offensive to nonbelievers, I also can see no reason to oppose a few minutes of silent meditation. During such a period those who want to pray can pray, and those who don't want to pray can think about baseball (which I often managed to do while reciting the Lord's Prayer), or anything else sectarian or nonsectarian they want to think about. If the teacher tries to make them pray, fire him. But there is absolutely nothing wrong—indeed there is great good—in asking young people to think quietly for a few moments about the meaning of it all. Yet many liberals see the prayer issue as one of the seminal battles of the enlightenment against the "hicks."

It is this contempt for the "hicks" that is the least appealing trait of the liberal intellectuals. Many of them, we have seen, don't really believe in democracy. Neoliberals do—we think a lot of those hicks are Huck Finns, with the common sense and good will to make the right choices if they are well informed. . . .

Neoliberalism Would Reform America's System of Government

Since experience is the best teacher of all, if we truly are going to reform the American system of government, we need to give more Americans experience in government. We need more politics, not less—more good people running for office. Unfortunately, the worst form of snobbery in America today is the smug assumption that politics and politicians are inherently bad.

If you think for a moment about the kind of choices we've had in recent elections, you'll realize why we must have a lot more good people pursuing political careers. This in turn means offering enough opportunities to attract people to a life in politics. Today a person who starts out in politics has a tiny field of opportunity in the federal government—congressman, senator, president, and just 2,000 appointive positions.

What if we opened hundreds of thousands of federal jobs to political appointees, replacing through normal attrition roughly half the federal government's 2.8 million civilian employees? Give the new people two-and-a-half year appointments, with a limit of five years on the time they would be permitted to remain in government.

This would bring people with real-world experience into government, attract more risk-takers not obsessed with job security and provide a legitimate reward for political participation. If we don't want a system that runs on money, then we have to offer something else. What is better to offer to the people who push the doorbells and hand out the leaflets than the opportunity to participate in putting into effect the programs they have campaigned for? Their reward would be legitimate because the unqualified would not profit from it. Your sister Susie who can't type 50 words a minute would not be allowed to get that government typing job no matter how hard she worked in your campaign.

Because the jobs would be limited to a few years, we also would be constantly sending back into the ranks of the voting public people who have learned firsthand why Washington doesn't work and who have nothing to lose from speaking out about the reforms that are needed. . . .

Restoring Power

There is no question, however, that restoring power to our elected officials does mean we have to watch them more carefully. That's why we need intelligent and diligent reporting, and that's why I would keep roughly half of government positions in the civil service. That leaves someone there to blow the whistle when the politicians go wrong, as sometimes they are bound to do. Civil servants would also provide continuity and institutional memory that would otherwise be lacking. But surely 50 percent can do that and still leave the other jobs to provide incentives for people to participate in politics and a dramatic increase in the number of people who understand the government.

If this approach had been in effect for even a decade, we would have a nation far better equipped to appraise the budget cuts that are said to be needed, who would have the sophistication to know exactly where to find them. We would have people in government who, because they'd spent most of their lives on the outside, would have genuine empathy for the problems of those on the outside. The lack of such empathy has been the most glaring deficiency of the bureaucracy in Washington.

What is the evidence that a system of democratic accountability would work better than the unaccountable civil service we have now? Those who were alive in the 1930s will remember that the post office delivered your packages intact and your letters on time, twice a day in fact. That postal system was political. If your mail didn't come on time you could complain to your congressman, and he would arrange for a new postmaster if he wanted to be reelected. The postal system became progressively less political in subsequent years and became completely nonpolitical in 1968. What has happened to your mail? What happens when you complain now? You probably don't even bother, which is why the present bureaucracy is so discouraging to democracy—the citizen who speaks up knows he is wasting his time. He calls Federal Express instead. . . .

Other positions taken in the past by *The Washington Monthly* are now becoming respectable wisdom. One is that liberals should not content themselves with merrily opposing increases in defense spending but should find out on what weapons money is being wasted and on what weapons more should be spent. In other words, identify both the turkeys and today's equivalents of Britain's Spitfire in World War II, the weapons that we need to survive. Another is that the insanity defense is itself insane and that violent criminals, sane or insane, should be locked up on the basis of the danger they pose to society. . . .

Conclusion

So we've traveled some of the way along the path. And that's good. But, frankly, I doubt if we'll make it the rest of the way without a rebirth of patriotism, a rebirth of devotion to the interests of the national community, of the conviction that we're all in this together and that therefore fair play and justice for everyone is the vital concern for us all. Robert McElvaine captured the model that should guide us in *Down and Out: Letters From the Forgotten Man in the Great Depression:*

"In letters that 'ordinary' Americans wrote during the 1930s, the overwhelming emphasis was upon themes of fairness and the necessity of justice. 'We are Poor People,' a group of Maryland WPA workers wrote to President Franklin D. Roosevelt in 1936, 'but we are human. We wish to be treated that way.' They went on to say, 'We feel you'll give us justice.' Similar sentiments were echoed in thousands of Depression-era letters. 'I knows and think that you feels our care and means right,' and anonymous correspondent wrote to F.D.R. in 1935, 'and you will do what is right if you knows the suffering of the people.' . . .

"The evidence that the major—although certainly not the exclusive—thrust of the current generation is toward extreme egotisical individualism is abundant. But the shift in values is not absolute. In all eras—and in most individuals—selfishness and compassion coexist. It is the mix of the two that varies. There is a tendency for the former to be more prevalent among the affluent, particularly if they are still on the rise or their positions are threatened. . . .

"Seen in this light, the basic difference between the dominant values of the 1930s and the 1980s is that much of the middle class in the earlier period identified with the poor, whereas the bulk of Middle America now aspires to become like the rich. The Joads of *The Grapes of Wrath* sought survival and a decent life; the Joneses seek not merely to keep up with each other; but to emulate the Rockefellers to whatever extent possible." . . .

In many ways life was much tougher in the thirties than it is today, but there was, incredibly enough, a lot more sunshine in the soul and a lot more laughter in the land. That spirit is the heart of neoliberalism. Without it, we will never overcome the politics of self-righteous, self-pitying interest groups. With it, we can begin to listen to one another, rebuild community, and take the risks that can produce the just and prosperous democratic society we all want.

Recognizing Stereotypes

A *stereotype* is an oversimplified or exaggerated description. It can apply to things or people and can be favorable or unfavorable. Quite often stereotyped beliefs about racial, religious, and national groups are insulting and oversimplified. They are usually based on misinformation or a lack of information.

Stereotyping grows out of our prejudices. When we stereotype someone, we are prejudging him or her. Consider the following example: Mr. X is convinced that all Mexicans are lazy, sloppy, and careless people. The Diaz family, a family a Mexicans, happen to be his next-door neighbors. One evening, upon returning home from work, Mr. X notices that the garbage pails in the Diaz driveway are overturned and that the rubbish is scattered over the driveway. He immediately says to himself: "Isn't that just like those lazy, sloppy, and careless Mexicans?" The possibility that a group of neighborhood vandals or a pack of stray dogs may be responsible for the mess never enters his mind. Why not? Simply because he has prejudged all Mexicans and will keep his stereotype consistent with his prejudice.

Examine carefully the following statements. Most are taken from the viewpoints in this book. Some have other origins. *Mark S for any statement that is an example of stereotyping. Mark N for any statement that is not an example of stereotyping. Mark U if you are undecided about any statement.*

If you are doing this activity as a member of a class or group, compare your answers with those of other class or group members. Be able to defend your answers. You may discover that others will come to different conclusions than you. Listening to the reasons others present for their answers may give you valuable insights into recognizing stereotypes.

If you are reading this book alone, ask others if they agree with your answers. You too will find this interaction very valuable.

> S = *stereotype*
> N = *not a stereotype*
> U = *undecided*

1. Political conservatives are opposed to the social security system.

2. Liberals, as a group, tend to be more sympathetic to the needs and desires of the poor and minorities.

3. Conservatives dress and act more conservatively than liberals.

4. Members of the American Nazi Party and the Ku Klux Klan are racists.

5. It is Christianity, after all, that has formed our ideas of law.

6. The liberal wants a state in which the lower and middle classes bear the brunt of all social change, while the liberals sit back with their union pay, or university pay, or inherited pay.

7. Liberal politicians favor welfare programs and make-work jobs that keep the poor dependent on liberal politicans.

8. The conservative Republican values system instinctively identifies with the well-to-do, those successful achievers or inheritors of the free enterprise society.

9. All blacks in America favor the welfare system.

10. Conservatives do not favor quick change for they fear it may bring negative results.

11. Conservatives stress authority, seeing true freedom as possible only within an ordered society that guides and limits the baser human instincts.

12. Extreme liberal thinkers are communist sympathizers.

Periodical Bibliography

The following list of periodical articles deals with the subject matter of this chapter.

The American Spectator	"On the Condition of Liberalism," April 1985.
Gar Alperovitz	"The Coming Break in Liberal Consciousness," *Christianity & Crisis*, March 3, 1986.
Business Week	"The Neo-Liberals Push Their Own Brand of Reform," January 31, 1983.
John Brown Childs	"The Schism in Liberal Thought: A Transition from Social Liberalism to Socialism?" *USA Today*, March 1981.
Commonweal	"Paths to a New Liberalism," December 5, 1980.
Edward L. Erickson	"Liberalism and the Morality of Freedom," *Free Inquiry*, Summer 1981.
Thomas Ferguson & Joel Rogers	"The Myth of America's Turn to the Right," *The Atlantic Monthly*, May 1986.
Thomas Ferguson & Joel Rogers	"Neoliberals and Democrats," *The Nation*, June 26, 1982.
Tom Hayden	"The Future Politics of Liberalism," *The Nation*, February 21, 1981.
John Judis	"Neoliberals," *The Progressive*, October 1982.
Morton Kondracke & Michael A. Scully	"Liberalism's Brave Neo World? Two Views," *Public Opinion*, April/May 1982.
Nicholas Lemann	"Values, Personal Choice, and the Failure of Liberalism," *The Washington Monthly*, December 1983.
Leslie Lenkowsky	"Does Neoliberalism Have a Future?" *Commentary*, March 1985.
Harry C. Meserve	"Confessions of a Crypto-Conservative," *The Churchman*, March 1983.
Malcolm Muggeridge	"Human Utopia: The Great Liberal Death Wish," *Christianity Today*, September 3, 1982.
Robert Nisbet	"The Quintessential Liberal," *Commentary*, September 1981.

Michael Novak — "A Genuinely New Liberal Spirit May Slowly Come to Prevail," *The Center Magazine*, January/February 1983.

Michael Novak — "What the Left Thinks the Right Thinks," *National Review*, March 28, 1986.

Charles Peters — "A Neoliberal's Manifesto," *The Washington Monthly*, May 1983.

Robert B. Reich — "The Liberal Promise of Prosperity," *The New Republic*, February 21, 1981.

Randall Rothenberg — "The Neoliberal Club," *Esquire*, February 1982.

Michael J. Sandel — "Morality and the Liberal Ideal," *The New Republic*, May 7, 1984.

Roger L. Shinn — "The End of a Liberal Dream," *Christianity & Crisis*, March 16, 1981.

Harry Stein — "Liberals: Their Own Worst Enemy," *The New York Times Magazine*, March 9, 1986.

Ben J. Wattenberg — "Charting the Economic Course: Can Neoliberalism Help?" *Public Opinion*, May 1982.

4

What Is
American Conservatism?

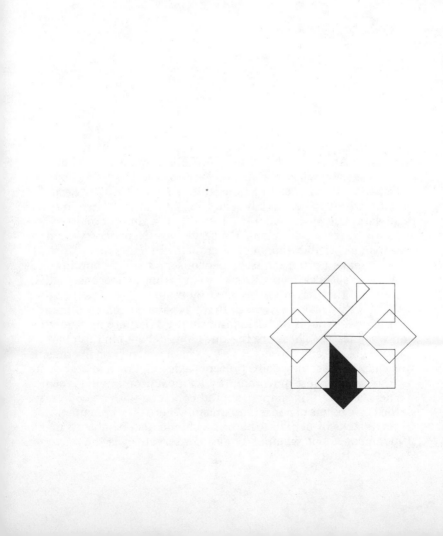

Chapter Preface

Conservatism, on the surface at least, seems to be the *ism* of the day in America. The White House is occupied by a conservative, and politicians are more likely to admit to being conservative than liberal. Leading magazines such as *The New Republic* and *Commentary*, once advocates of liberalism, have moved rightward. University faculties, formerly the almost exclusive domain of liberals, now claim conservatives. Neoconservatism is much more visible than neoliberalism. In fact, many former liberals make up the ranks of neoconservatism, prompting the movement's leader, Irving Kristol, to quip that "a neoconservative is a liberal that has been mugged by reality."

What is this basic movement that has gained such prominence in America? What is its basic philosophy? What are its strengths and weaknesses? These are the questions debated in this chapter by both liberals and conservatives. As in the chapter on liberalism, this chapter's last viewpoint presents a description and argument for the *ism*'s newest movement by its most prominent advocate.

The reader of this chapter should conclude with a good grasp of the basic tenets of conservatism and where they are vulnerable to the attacks of liberals. She or he should also be able to make a judgment about whether or not conservatism is the wave of America's future.

*"Conservatives uphold the principle of social
continuity. They prefer the devil they know to
the devil they don't know."*

The Principles
of Conservatism

Russell Kirk

Since the publication of his *The Conservative Mind* in 1953, a
history of Anglo-American thought and a detailed attack on
liberalism, Russell Kirk has been regarded as a prominent
spokesman for American conservatism. A prolific writer of
political essays, newspaper columns, and a variety of books, he
is currently editor of the conservative quarterly *The University
Bookman*. In the following viewpoint, taken from the introduction to Mr. Kirk's book *The Portable Conservative Reader*, he outlines
the basic principles of British and American Conservatism. Consistent with the viewpoint's concise and direct style, he concludes
by stating that "for the conservative, politics is the art of the possible, not the art of the ideal."

As you read, consider the following questions:

1. What is the "principal of prescription," and how does it
   relate to "rights in property"?
2. According to Mr. Kirk, how do conservatives view equality
   and the existence of different orders and classes?
3. In the author's opinion, how do conservatives view human
   nature?

Strictly speaking, conservatism is not a political system, and certainly not an ideology. In the phrase of H. Stuart Hughes, "Conservatism is the negation of ideology." Instead, conservatism is a way of looking at the civil social order. Although certain general principles held by most conservatives may be described, there exists wide variety in application of these ideas from age to age and country to country. . . .

For our present purpose, however, we may set down below several general principles upon which most eminent conservatives in some degree may be said to have agreed implicitly. The following first principles are best discerned in the theoretical and practical politics of British and American conservatives.

A Transcendent Moral Order

First, conservatives generally believe that there exists a transcendent moral order, to which we ought to try to conform the ways of society. A divine tactic, however dimly descried, is at work in human society. Such convictions may take the form of belief in "natural law" or may assume some other expression; but with few exceptions conservatives recognize the need for enduring moral authority. This conviction contrasts strongly with the liberals' utilitarian view of the state (most consistently expressed by Bentham's disciples), and with the radicals' detestation of theological postulates.

The Principle of Social Continuity

Second, conservatives uphold the principle of social continuity. They prefer the devil they know to the devil they don't know. Order and justice and freedom, they believe, are the artificial products of a long and painful social experience, the results of centuries of trial and reflection and sacrifice. Thus the body social is a kind of spiritual corporation, comparable to the church; it may even be called a community of souls. Human society is no machine, to be treated mechanically. The continuity, the lifeblood, of a society must not be interrupted. Burke's reminder of the social necessity for prudent change is in the minds of conservatives. But necessary change, they argue, ought to be gradual and discriminatory, never "unfixing old interests at once." Revolution slices through the arteries of a culture, a cure that kills.

The Principle of Prescription

Third, conservatives believe in what may be called the principle of prescription. "The wisdom of our ancestors" is one of the more important phrases in the writings of Burke; presumably Burke derived it from Richard Hooker. Conservatives sense that modern men and women are dwarfs on the shoulders of giants, able to see farther than their ancestors only because of the great stature of those who have preceded us in time. Therefore conservatives very frequently emphasize the importance of "prescription"—that is, of things established by immemorial usage, so "that the mind of man runneth not to the contrary." There exist rights of which the chief sanction is their antiquity—including rights in property, often. Similarly, our morals are prescriptive in great part. Conservatives argue that we are unlikely, we moderns, to make any brave new discoveries in morals or politics or taste. It is perilous to weigh every passing issue on the basis of private judgment and private rationality. "The individual is foolish, but the species is wise," Burke declared. In politics we do well to abide by precedent and precept and even prejudice, for "the great mysterious incorporation of the human race" has acquired habits, customs, and conventions of remote origin which are woven into the fabric of our social being; the innovator, in Santayana's phrase, never knows how near to the taproot of the tree he is hacking.

The Principle of Prudence

Fourth, conservatives are guided by their principle of prudence. Burke agrees with Plato that in the statesman, prudence is chief among virtues. Any public measure ought to be judged by its probable long-run consequences, not merely by temporary advantage or popularity. Liberals and radicals, the conservative holds, are imprudent: for they dash at their objectives without giving much heed to the risk of new abuses worse than the evils they hope to sweep away. Human society being complex, remedies cannot be simple if they are to be effective. The conservative declares that he acts only after sufficient reflection, having weighed the consequences. Sudden and slashing reforms are perilous as sudden and slashing surgery. The march of providence is slow; it is the devil who always hurries.

The Principle of Variety

Fifth, conservatives pay attention to the principle of variety. They feel affection for the proliferating intricacy of long-established social institutions and modes of life, as distinguished from the narrowing uniformity and deadening egalitarianism of radical systems. For the preservation of a healthy diversity in any civilization, there must survive orders and classes, differences in material condition, and many sorts of inequality. The only true forms of equality are equality in the Last Judgment and equality before a just court of law; all other attempts at leveling lead, at best, to social stagnation. Society longs for honest and able leadership; and if natural and institutional differences among people are destroyed, presently some tyrant or host of squalid oligarchs will create new forms of inequality. Similarly, conservatives uphold the institution of private property as productive of human variety: without private property, liberty is reduced and culture is impoverished.

The Principle of Imperfectibility

Sixth, conservatives are chastened by their principle of imperfectibility. Human nature suffers irremediably from certain faults, the convervatives know. Man being imperfect, no perfect social order ever can be created. Because of human restlessness, mankind would grow rebellious under any utopian domination, and would break out once more in violent discontent—or else expire of boredom. To aim for utopia is to end in disaster, the conservative says: we are not made for perfect things. All that we reasonably can expect is a tolerably ordered, just, and free society, in which some evils, maladjustments, and suffering continue to lurk. By proper attention to prudent reform, we may preserve and improve this tolerable order. But if the old institutional and moral safeguards of a nation are forgotten, then the anarchic impulses in man break loose: "the ceremony of innocence is drowned."

The Conservative Impulse

At bottom, then, conservatism is not a matter of economic interests and economic theories; not a matter of political advantages and political systems; not a matter of power or preferment. If we penetrate to the root, we discover that "conservatism" is a way of looking at the human condition. As a conservative Polish proverb puts it, "Old truths, old laws, old boots, old books, and old friends are the best." The conservative impulse is a man's desire to walk in the paths that his father followed; it is a woman's desire for the sureties of hearth and home.

Russell Kirk, *The Portable Conservative Reader*, 1982.

Such are six of the major premises of what Walter Bagehot, a century ago, called "reflective conservatism." To have set down some principal convictions of conservative thinkers, in the fashion above, may be misleading: for conservative thought is not a body of immutable secular dogmas. Our purpose here has been broad description, not fixed definition. If one requires a single sentence—why, let it be said that for the conservative, politics is the art of the possible, not the art of the ideal.

*"Conservatives are inclined to use the powers
of government to prevent change or to limit its
rate to whatever appeals to the more timid
mind."*

Why I Am Not
a Conservative

F.A. Hayek

In 1944, Friedrich Hayek's book *The Road to Serfdom*, was published in America. Reprinted by *Reader's Digest* and distributed by
the Book-of-the-Month Club, it sold over a million copies. Hayek,
an Austrian economist at the time, claimed that government planning and the control of economic activity led to the loss of freedom
and to eventual dictatorship. He pointed to Nazi Germany as an
example of his thesis. In 1960, he published an essay "Why I Am
Not a Conservative," attacking conservatism as lacking a coherent
set of principles and for being too reliant on the powers of the
State to achieve its goals. The following viewpoint is taken from
that essay.

As you read, consider the following questions:

1. Why does the author claim conservatism offers no alternative to the direction society is moving?
2. Why does he make the claim that "it seems to be so much
   easier for the repentant socialist to find a new spiritual
   home in the conservative fold than in the liberal"?
3. What argument does he make to support his claim that
   conservatism has an antidemocratic strain?

F.A. Hayek, "Why I Am Not a Conservative," from *The Constitution of Liberty*. Chicago:
The University of Chicago Press, 1960. Reprinted with permission.

Conservatism proper is a legitimate, probably necessary, and certainly widespread attitude of opposition to drastic change. It has, since the French Revolution, for a century and a half played an important role in European politics. Until the rise of socialism its opposite was liberalism. There is nothing corresponding to this conflict in the history of the United States, because what in Europe was called "liberalism" was here the common tradition on which the American polity had been built: thus the defender of the American tradition was a liberal in the European sense. This already existing confusion was made worse by the recent attempt to transplant to America the European type of conservatism, which, being alien to the American tradition, has acquired a somewhat odd character. And some time before this, American radicals and socialists began calling themselves "liberals.". . .

Conservatism Offers No Alternative

Let me now state what seems to me the decisive objection to any conservatism which deserves to be called such. It is that by its very nature it cannot offer an alternative to the direction in which we are moving. It may succeed by its resistance to current tendencies in slowing down undesirable developments, but, since it does not indicate another direction, it cannot prevent their continuance. It has, for this reason, invariably been the fate of conservatism to be dragged along a path not of its own choosing. The tug of war between conservatives and progressives can only affect the speed, not the direction, of contemporary developments. But, though there is need for a "brake on the vehicle of progress," I personally cannot be content with simply helping to apply the brake. . . .

The picture generally given of the relative position of the three parties does more to obscure than to elucidate their true relations. They are usually represented as different positions on a line, with the socialists on the left, the conservatives on the right, and the liberals somewhere in the middle. Nothing could be more misleading. If we want a diagram, it would be more appropriate to arrange them in a triangle with the conservatives occupying one corner, with the socialists pulling towards the second and the liberals towards the third. But, as the socialists have for a long time been able to pull harder, the conservatives have tended to follow the socialist rather than the liberal direction and have adopted at appropriate intervals of time those ideas made respectable by radical propaganda. It has been regularly the conservatives who have compromised with socialism and stolen its thunder. Advocates of the Middle Way, with no goal of their own, conservatives have been guided by the belief that the truth must lie somewhere between the extremes—with the result that they have shifted their position every time a more extreme movement appeared on either wing.

The position which can be rightly described as conservative at any time depends, therefore, on the direction of existing tendencies. Since the development during the last decades has been generally in a socialist direction, it may seem that both conservatives and liberals have been mainly intent on retarding that movement. But the main point about liberalism is that it wants to go elsewhere, not to stand still. Though today the contrary impression may sometimes be caused by the fact that there was a time when liberalism was more widely accepted and some of its objectives closer to being achieved, it has never been a backward-looking doctrine. There has never been a time when liberal ideals were fully realized and when liberalism did not look forward to further improvement of institutions. Liberalism is not adverse to evolution and change; and where spontaneous change has been smothered by government control, it wants a great deal of change of policy. So far as much of current governmental action is concerned, there is in the present world very little reason for the liberal to wish to preserve things as they are. It would seem to the liberal, indeed, that what is most urgently needed in most parts of the world is a thorough sweeping away of the obstacles to free growth.

Conservatism's Fatal Flaw

Let me now state what seems to me the decisive objection to any conservatism which deserves to be called such. It is that by its very nature it cannot offer an alternative to the direction in which we are moving. It may succeed by its resistance to current tendencies in slowing down undesirable developments, but, since it does not indicate another direction, it cannot prevent their continuance. It has, for this reason, invariably been the fate of conservatism to be dragged along a path not of its own choosing.

F.A. Hayek, *The Constitution of Liberty*, 1960.

This difference between liberalism and conservatism must not be obscured by the fact that in the United States it is still possible to defend individual liberty by defending long-established institutions. To the liberal they are valuable not mainly because they are long-established or because they are American but because they correspond to the ideals which he cherishes. . . .

A Fear of Change

As has often been acknowledged by conservative writers, one of the fundamental traits of the conservative attitude is a fear of change, a timid distrust of the new as such, while the liberal position is based on courage and confidence, on a preparedness to let change run its course even if we cannot predict where it will lead.

There would not be much to object to if the conservatives merely disliked too rapid change in institutions and public policy; here the case for caution and slow process is indeed strong. But the conservatives are inclined to use the powers of government to prevent change or to limit its rate to whatever appeals to the more timid mind. In looking forward, they lack the faith in the spontaneous forces of adjustment which makes the liberal accept changes without apprehension, even though he does not know how the necessary adaptations will be brought about. It is, indeed, part of the liberal attitude to assume that, especially in the economic field, the self-regulating forces of the market will somehow bring about the required adjustments to new conditions, although no one can foretell how they will do this in a particular instance. There is perhaps no single factor contributing so much to people's frequent reluctance to let the market work as their inability to conceive how some necessary balance, between demand and supply, between exports and imports, or the like, will be brought about without deliberate control. The conservative feels safe and content only if he is assured that some higher wisdom watches and supervises change, only if he knows that some authority is charged with keeping the change "orderly."

A Fondness For Authority

This fear of trusting uncontrolled social forces is closely related to two other characteristics of conservatism: its fondness for authority and its lack of understanding of economic forces. Since it distrusts both abstract theories and general principles, it neither understands those spontaneous forces on which a policy of freedom relies nor possesses a basis for formulating principles of policy. Order appears to the conservatives as the result of the continuous attention of authority, which, for this purpose, must be allowed to do what is required by the particular circumstances and not be tied to rigid rule. A commitment to principles presupposes an understanding of the general forces by which the efforts of society are co-ordinated, but it is such a theory of society and especially of the economic mechanism that conservatism conspicuously lacks. So unproductive has conservatism been in producing a general conception of how a social order is maintained that its modern votaries, in trying to construct a theoretical foundation, invariably find themselves appealing almost exclusively to authors who regarded themselves as liberal. Macaulay, Tocqueville, Lord Acton, and Lecky certainly considered themselves liberals, and with justice; and even Edmund Burke remained an Old Whig to the end and would have shuddered at the thought of being regarded as a Tory.

Let me return, however, to the main point, which is the characteristic complacency of the conservative towards the action of established authority and his prime concern that this authority be not weakened rather than that its power be kept within bounds. This is difficult to reconcile with the preservation of liberty. In general, it can probably be said that the conservative does not object to coercion or arbitrary power so long as it is used for what he regards as the right purposes. He believes that if government is in the hands of decent men, it ought not be too much restricted by rigid rules. Since he is essentially opportunist and lacks principles, his main hope must be that the wise and the good will rule—not merely by example, as we all must wish, but by authority given to them and enforced by them. Like the socialist, he is less concerned with the problem of how the powers of government should be limited than with that of who wields them; and, like the socialist, he regards himself as entitled to force the value he holds on other people.

A Lack of Political Principles

When I say that the conservative lacks principles, I do not mean to suggest that he lacks moral conviction. The typical conservative is indeed usually a man of very strong moral convictions. What I mean is that he has no political principles which enable him to work with people whose moral values differ from his own for a political order in which both can obey their convictions. It is the recognition of such principles that permits the coexistence of different sets of values, that makes it possible to build a peaceful society with a minimum of force. The acceptance of such principles means that we agree to tolerate much that we dislike. There are many values of the conservative which appeal to me more than those of the socialists; yet for a liberal the importance he personally attaches to specific goals is not sufficient justification for forcing others to serve them. I have little doubt that some of my conservative friends will be shocked by what they will regard as "concessions" to modern views that I have made in Part III of *The Constitution of Liberty*. But, though I may dislike some of the measures concerned as much as they do and might vote against them, I know of no general principles to which I could appeal to persuade those of a different view that those measures are not permissible in the general kind of society which we both desire. To live and work successfully with others requires more than faithfulness to one's concrete aims. It requires an intellectual commitment to a type of order in which, even on issues which to one are fundamental, others are allowed to pursue different ends.

It is for this reason that to the liberal neither moral nor religious ideals are proper objects of coercion, while both conservatives and socialists recognize no such limits. I sometimes feel that the most conspicuous attribute of liberalism that distinguishes it as much from conservatism as from socialism is the view that moral beliefs concerning matters of conduct which do not directly interfere with the protected sphere of other persons do not justify coercion. This

155

may also explain why it seems to be so much easier for the repentant socialist to find a new spiritual home in the conservative fold than in the liberal.

In the last resort, the conservative position rests on the belief that in any society there are recognizably superior persons whose inherited standards and values and position ought to be protected and who should have a greater influence on public affairs than others. The liberal, of course, does not deny that there are some superior people—he is not an egalitarian—but he denies that anyone has authority to decide who these superior people are.

"Oh, I'm in favor of progress all right— what I can't stand is change!"

While the conservative inclines to defend a particular established hierarchy and wishes authority to protect the status of those whom he values, the liberal feels that no respect for established values can justify the resort to privilege or monopoly or any other coercive power of the state in order to shelter such people against the forces of economic change. Though he is fully aware of the important role that cultural and intellectual elites have played in the evolution of civilization, he also believes that these elites have to prove themselves by their capacity to maintain their position under the same rules that apply to all others.

Closely connected with this is the usual attitude of the conservative to democracy. I have made it clear that I do not regard majority rule as an end but merely as a means, or perhaps even as the least evil of those forms of government from which we have to choose. But I believe that the conservatives deceive themselves when they blame the evils of our time on democracy. The chief evil is unlimited government, and nobody is qualified to wield unlimited power. The powers which modern democracy possesses would be even more intolerable in the hands of some small elite.

Admittedly, it was only when power came into the hands of the majority that further limitation of the power of government was thought unnecessary. In this sense democracy and unlimited government are connected. But it is not democracy but unlimited government that is objectionable, and I do not see why the people should not learn to limit the scope of majority rule as well as that of any other form of government. At any rate, the advantages of democracy as a method of peaceful change and of political education seem to be so great compared with those of any other system that I can have no sympathy with the antidemocratic strain of conservatism. It is not who governs but what government is entitled to do that seems to me the essential problem.

That the conservative opposition to too much government control is not a matter of principle but is concerned with the particular aims of government is clearly shown in the economic sphere. Conservatives usually oppose collectivist and directivist measures in the industrial field, and here the liberal will often find allies in them. But at the same time conservatives are usually protectionists and have frequently supported socialist measures in agriculture. Indeed, though the restrictions which exist today in industry and commerce are mainly the result of socialist views, the equally important restrictions in agriculture were usually introduced by conservatives at an even earlier date. And in their efforts to discredit free enterprise many conservative leaders have vied with the socialists.

A Fear of New Ideas

I have already referred to the differences between conservatism and liberalism in the purely intellectual field, but I must return to them because the characteristic conservative attitude here not only is a serious weakness of conservatism but tends to harm any cause which allies itself with it. Conservatives feel instinctively that it is new ideas more than anything else that cause change. But, from its point of view rightly, conservatism fears new ideas because it has no distinctive principles of its own to oppose to them; and, by its distrust of theory and its lack of imagination concerning anything except that which experience has already proved, it deprives itself of the weapons needed in the struggle of ideas. Unlike liberalism with its fundamental belief in the long-range power of ideas, conservatism is bound by the stock of ideas inherited at a given time. And since it does not really believe in the power of argument, its last resort is generally a claim to superior wisdom, based on some self-arrogated superior quality.

This difference shows itself most clearly in the different attitudes of the two traditions to the advance of knowledge. Though the liberal certainly does not regard all change as progress, he does regard the advance of knowledge as one of the chief aims of human effort and expects from it the gradual solution of such problems and difficulties as we can hope to solve. Without preferring the new merely because it is new, the liberal is aware that it is of the essence of human achievement that it produces something new; and he is prepared to come to terms with new knowledge, whether he likes its immediate effects or not.

Personally, I find that the most objectionable feature of the conservative attitude is its propensity to reject well-substantiated new knowledge because it dislikes some of the consequences which seem to follow from it—or, to put it bluntly, its obscurantism. I will not deny that scientists as much as others are given to fads and fashions and that we have much reason to be cautious in accepting the conclusions that they draw their latest theories. But the reasons for our reluctance must themselves be rational and must be kept separate from our regret that the new theories upset our cherished beliefs. I can have little patience with those who oppose, for instance, the theory of evolution or what are called "mechanistic" explanations of the phenomena of life simply because of certain moral consequences which at first seem to follow from these theories, and still less with those who regard it as irreverent or impious to ask certain questions at all. By refusing to face the facts, the conservative only weakens his own position. Frequently the conclusions which rationalist presumption draws from new scientific insights do not at all follow from them. But only by actively taking part in the elaboration of the consequences of new discoveries do we learn whether or not they fit into our world picture and, if so, how. Should our moral beliefs really prove to be dependent on factual assumptions shown to be incorrect, it would be hardly moral to defend them by refusing to acknowledge facts.

Conservatism's Strident Nationalism

Connected with the conservative distrust of the new and the strange is its hostility to internationalism and its proneness to a strident nationalism. Here is another source of its weakness in the struggle of ideas. It cannot alter the fact that the ideas which are changing our civilization respect no boundaries. But refusal to acquaint one's self with new ideas merely deprives one of the power of effectively countering them when necessary. The growth of ideas is an international process, and only those who fully take part in the discussion will be able to exercise a significant influence. It is no real argument to say that an idea is un-American, un-British, or un-German, nor is a mistaken or vicious ideal better for having been conceived by one of our compatriots. . . .

I need hardly say that nationalism of this sort is something very different from patriotism and that an aversion to nationalism is fully compatible with a deep attachment to national traditions. But the fact that I prefer and feel reverence for some of the traditions of society may need not be the cause of hostility to what is strange and different.

Only at first does it seem paradoxical that the anti-internationalism of the conservatives is so frequently associated with imperialism. But the more a person dislikes the strange and thinks his own ways superior, the more he tends to regard it as his mission to "civilize" others—not by the voluntary and unhampered intercourse which the liberal favors, but by bringing them the blessings of efficient government. It is significant that here again we frequently find the conservatives joining hands with the socialists against the liberals. . . .

Conclusion

What I have described as the liberal position shares with conservatism a distrust of reason to the extent that the liberal is very much aware that we do not know all the answers and that he is not sure that the answers he has are certainly the right ones or even that we can find all the answers. He also does not disdain to seek assistance from whatever non-rational institutions or habits have proved their worth. The liberal differs from the conservative in his willingness to face this ignorance and to admit how little we know, without claiming the authority of supernatural sources of knowledge where his reason fails him. It has to be admitted that in some respects the liberal is fundamentally a skeptic—but it seems to require a certain degree of diffidence to let others seek their happiness in their own fashion and to adhere consistently to that tolerance which is an essential characteristic of liberalism.

"Liberals determine policy on the basis of the perceived situation, the immediate need. . . . Conservatives, on the other hand, look to values and absolutes to direct them."

The Case for Modern Conservatism

James G. Watt

James Watt has served in various government and political positions during the administrations of the last six presidents. The most recent was as Secretary of the Interior during the first three years of the Reagan administration. In the following viewpoint, taken from the book *The Courage of a Conservative*, Watt addresses modern conservatives, asking them to apply conservative principles in reforming America's welfare state. He claims America is at a crisis point, pitting freedom-loving individuals against the domination of government bureaucracies. The solution, in the author's opinion, is to return to the basic conservative values which form the core of American democracy.

As you read, consider the following questions:

1. What point does the author make in claiming "the contest between liberals and conservatives is a moral battle"?
2. Why does he refer to his cause as "the modern conservative movement"?
3. What reference point does he use in distinguishing between the terms "liberal" and "conservative"?

James G. Watt with Doug Wead, *The Courage of a Conservative*. New York: Simon & Schuster, Inc., 1985. Copyright © 1985 by James G. Watt and Doug Wead. Reprinted by permission of SIMON & SCHUSTER, Inc.

There is an intense battle raging in this land. It can be described in political terms, theological expressions or economic equations because it is being fought in the halls of government, in the churches and in the marketplace. Its outcome will determine how we and our children will be governed in the twenty-first century.

The focus of the battle has become the dignity of the individual versus the domination of government. Will America have a society of giant bureaucratic institutions, in both the public and the private sector, institutions that will have increasing power to control the economic and social behavior of the individual? Or will we have a society that restores and respects the dignity of individuals, so that they can enjoy their spiritual freedom and political liberty?

Since its beginnings in the early 1960s, the modern conservative movement has been warning the American people that we are at a crossroads. A massive, powerful government bureaucracy egged on by selfish special-interest groups is encroaching on the rights of the individual. . . .

Limited Role for Government

Then what is the conservative alternative? If government cannot solve all the problems of the people, who will? Shall we let the disadvantaged starve? Shall we allow confidence men to promote phony cures for cancer? Should all federal regulations be cut, all subsidies to the needy stopped? Should the federal government pull out and leave volunteer organizations, the states and local communities holding the bag for everything? Shall we return to the separatism of colonial America?

Of course not. Modern conservatives recognize that circumstances are different today from what they were in the 1770s. We would not repeal the Social Security system or eliminate welfare payments to the truly needy. We acknowledge that a kind of second revolution took place when, under Franklin Roosevelt, the federal government stepped in and took charge during the emergency of the Great Depression. We applaud the ability of a centralized government to respond quickly in a modern age when national problems arise. We applaud the federal government's role in helping to check racial discrimination, for example.

That is why I refer to our movement as the *modern* conservative movement. In America's past, we conservatives of today would hardly be considered conservative at all. We are conservative now about the degree of federal involvement. At best, we see excessive government as promoting a failed economic policy, financially defrauding the very disadvantaged people it had promised to help. At worst, we see excessive government as a threat to the spiritual freedom and individual liberty of its citizens.

Modern conservatives have not called for the dismantling of the entire government bureaucracy. But we have called for a serious pruning, and, far beyond any technical adjustment here or there,

'LET'S FACE IT - YOU AND I MAKE A GREAT TEAM'

Don Hess © 1980, *St. Louis Globe-Democrat*. Reprinted with permission Los Angeles Times Syndicate.

we are seeking to recapture the original American idea.

The modern conservative takes issue with the suggestion that the American system is flawed or corrupt and requires massive governmental intervention to right it. We have no romantic illusions about a worldwide Socialist movement that manifests itself in its newly formed governments with mass murders of millions, and in its older established governments with inefficient industry, creating products that don't work and shortages for its workers. Conservatives feel no compulsion to borrow economic solutions from countries that can't even supply their own people with basic needs. We believe in the original American idea of guaranteeing dignity for the individual through political liberty and spiritual freedom. We seek a counterrevolution to recapture the best of that idea.

162

America is at a crossroads. With each election, she is taking another step. We conservatives argue that her roots are good, that we can trust and should conserve the original idea. There is no other country with our spiritual freedom and individual liberty. Let the Swedes nationalize their banks to resolve a temporary economic crisis. Let the French government experiment with socialism and take ownership of its steel factories. Let the British tax their corporations at an 80 percent rate and socialize their medicine. Let the Cubans and Nicaraguans protect their peoples from the "evils of religion" and use government to fight—and, in the case of the Cubans, actually close—their churches and synagogues.

America is one of a kind. She should not be insecure and should not let her imperfections panic her into mimicking inferior models. . . .

Who Is Right?

The contest between liberals and conservatives is a moral battle. It is a contest over who is right and who is wrong. There are many liberals who would take exception to this statement. They complain that it smacks too much of religion. They would say we conservatives are always trying to moralize and express issues in terms of good and bad. Still, no matter how they may protest, this is the truth: the battle is over who is right.

When a staunch liberal says he is for the nuclear freeze, it is not because he wants to get elected. He would support the nuclear freeze even if he only got one vote. He believes it is right, that it is a moral outrage to continue to build weapons to blow up the world.

When a true conservative says that a nuclear freeze wouldn't work unless the Russians actually complied with it, he is not just posturing to get into office. He would say the same thing even if it meant losing his seat in the Senate. He would point out the moral difference between the West and the Marxist totalitarian governments, with their history of mass exterminations in Cambodia and China and Russia, and their outrageous use of drugs to alter the minds of their own dissidents. The conservative would be making a moral argument about the need to remain vigilant and to protect the sovereignty of our free nation.

When liberals say they are pro-choice in the abortion debate, they are not simply pulling a cause out of a hat. Liberals would contend that it is immoral for wealthy women to be able to pay for abortions if they want them, while the government does not provide funds for that service to poorer women. Liberals want a woman to have the freedom, regardless of economics, to give or deny birth to a baby as she desires.

Conservatives, on the other hand, want to protect the rights of the unborn baby. It is a clear moral issue. Does society protect the rights of the unborn or the desires of the mother? . . .

It is quite absurd to say that morality is irrelevant to political philosophy, that government is simply an exercise in accounting, that it is all mathematical. And no matter how popular it may be at the moment, the belief that "policy is dictated by circumstances, it doesn't really matter who is in power" is an attempt to avoid moral responsibility. . . .

Conservative or Liberal About What?

What do I mean when I say liberal and conservative? There really must be a definition of terms, a point of reference. There must be something about which to be liberal or conservative or moderate.

In recent years, liberals have argued and written as if the point of reference in this whole debate is *whether* to meet the needs of people. This view has been popularized by sympathetic media. It is difficult to watch a sincere and well-intentioned television newsman reciting unemployent figures without feeling some anger toward anyone in government who would hesitate to offer help. The intended implication of this view is that liberals are liberal in responding to the needs of people, moderates are reluctant, and conservatives are selfish and uncaring.

This is absurd. If the needs of people were the point of reference, we wouldn't even be using the terms *liberal* or *moderate* or *conservative.* We would all be "liberals." How could anyone be moderate or reluctant to help poor people or victims of discrimination? What virtue is there in being moderately concerned about people? To be conservative in responding to such need would be unconscionable and cruel. If the needs of people were what this debate were all about, I would be "liberal" in an instant, for I am committed to the dignity, freedom and liberty of the individual. People are the important factor, not institutions or corporations or stone monuments or grassy malls or even what is said in history books.

In the philosophical war between conservatives and liberals, there is a battle over semantics and words and terminology. We are not debating whether to meet the needs of people, or whether there should be discrimination or poverty or peace. Needs are not the point of reference about which we are liberal or conservative. The distorted claim that liberals are the only ones who care about people has been used to defeat the conservative position. Although many Americans have been misled by this argument, they have begun to recognize the deception promoted by evening newscasters who espouse liberal views about "who really cares about the people." When millions upon millions of Americans voted for a conservative candidate, it was not because they weren't concerned, for many are themselves suffering discrimination or facing economic difficulties. They voted precisely because they

Liberalism's Tyranny of Virtue

Now almost everything we liberals did in the past thirty years was colored with virtue. It's what I call the "tyranny of virtue." You can't vote against aid to the handicapped; you can't vote against rat-control programs in the big city; you can't vote against the enormous development of medical services. Your conscience won't let you. You can't vote against Medicare or Medicaid. You can't vote against free school lunches.

When you add all of these things up, and put them all together in a package—when you set down the old package of privileges, like veterans' bonuses or veterans' pensions, or the farmers' protected prices, and the banks get their bit of it and the big aircraft companies get their bit of it—you have a society which is more dependent on the largess of the federal government than we liberals ever conceived of in the beginning. . . .

Here in New York City, at Sixty-third Street, we are building the most magnificent subway station in the USA. In one of the clauses, I think, of the Rehabilitation Act, it says that no federal funds will go to a mass transit project unless it provides ramps, lifts, and elevators for the handicapped.

The subway stations over here at the corner of Sixty-third and Lexington will be a dream of ramps, lifts, elevators. That's lovely—except for the fact that the poor handicapped, once they got down safely into that subway, will have no place to go. Because they can't get out at Thirty-fourth Street, they can't get out at Chambers Street, they can't get out at Far Rockaway, they can't get out in the Bronx. Because it would take untold millions to equip all the hundreds of subway stations in New York with ramps and elevators.

So here we have this enormous expenditure for building this magnificent subway station, and then all that it'll do is ride around the circuit and come out at the same place. Is there a politician in New York who would dare to say that's a waste of money? But it would be cheaper to take the handicapped by cab or by bus to their jobs in the morning than to put in the installation over there. It will be one of the most expensive in the USA. This subway system—this stretch of subway over here between Central Park and the East River—will probably cost us as much as one of these spectacular aircraft carriers.

We've created a nation of dependents. How to unravel that, no one knows. How to pay for it, no one knows. That gets us to a social, cultural, economic crisis the like of which we haven't seen since 1932.

Theodore H. White, *Society*, July/August 1983.

do care, and they believe the conservative has the best answers to ensure individual liberty and economic prosperity.

Then what is the point of reference? And where do the terms *liberal* and *conservative* come from? The point of reference is *how* to meet the needs of people and the constitutional limitations on the role of government. Liberals will allow for a very liberal interpretation of the Constitution when they believe it will help them meet the needs of the people. They are willing to change the forms of law and government to meet immediate needs. Moderates are much more cautious, and we conservatives can be downright tough and very protective of the constitutional limits on the role of government. We believe that the basic American system has worked well. The constitutional rights of political, religious and economic freedoms have given Americans the highest quality of life in the world. Like the early revolutionary Americans, we conservatives fear that self-righteous, unlimited government, no matter how well intentioned, will eventually abuse its powers and everyone's freedom. We conservatives consider ourselves the champions of individual liberty in the battle against the centralization of power.

Supporters of Strength

To be sure, we conservatives can be quite generous when it comes to financing the responsibilities that the Constitution clearly allows. After great debate, our founding fathers determined that a national army was necessary to "provide for the common defense." We are big supporters of a strong America. Yet we conservatives can be very cautious about other, more recent, government responsibilities that had been considered unconstitutional for nearly two centuries but in recent years have been determined by liberal Congresses and courts to be legitimate. Whenever possible, conservatives will seek to restrain government power, or at least direct it in such a way that it will involve the private sector and give people incentives to deal with their own problems in order to protect their traditional values, individual dignity and freedom.

So the point of reference is the role of government in meeting the needs of people. That—and not who has the most compassion—is the subject of the debate.

Both moderates and liberals determine policy on the basis of the perceived situation, the immediate need. They are willing to compromise the traditional restraints of the American system if it will satisfactorily address the need at hand. Conservatives, on the other hand, look to values and absolutes to direct them.

There is a theological parallel to this political debate. Conservative politicians attract conservative theologians precisely because both look to traditional values and absolutes for direction. Some scholars suggest that the political and the religious

166

share the same absolutes and values. It is true that the structure of American government borrows much from its Judeo-Christian tradition.

There is a similar parallel with liberals. Modern liberal theologians who have come to question the absolutes of their own faith have much in common with modern political liberals who have become quite critical and self-conscious of the hypocritical role they believe that America plays in the world. Both groups would view themselves as iconoclastic, even daring, in their willingness to defy tradition. They say, "Tell me the problem. Don't tell me the rules." It is situational ethics for liberals in either case.

The Debate Moves Left

With each decade the debate about the role of government has become increasingly liberal because of the power of the liberal Establishment, the Congress, big business, the unions and the media. . . .

Of course, some people would not accept this assessment. They would say that there has been a shift to the Right among the general population. Surveys do show more and more voters identifying themselves as conservatives. But that is not so much because the voters are moving Right as it is because the debate is moving Left. As the liberal leaders become more and more liberal, they are leaving more and more people behind them. Some people have become conservative by default. They just won't move any farther Left.

A case could be made that we conservatives of today are so liberal by yesterday's standards that a New Dealer would feel quite at home with us. The big debate twenty-five years ago concerned federal aid to education and whether it would lead to federal controls. Today, by contrast, we are debating whether nine-year-olds violate federal law when they pray over their lunches in a school cafeteria, or whether homosexual teachers have the right to advocate their life-style to their students. Forty-five years ago, liberals contended that federal welfare was desirable for the truly needy and could serve as a transitional support to help capable but temporarily unlucky workers back into the work force. This is exactly the philosophy that we modern conservatives would subscribe to today. But what is the welfare system like now? And when it comes to the contemporary problem of criminal justice, a Harvard professor recently said it best. "There are no more liberals on the crime and law-and-order issue . . . they've all been mugged."

So when I write about conservatives, remember I am writing about modern conservatives. We are probably the most liberal conservatives the nation has ever known. In the context of American history, some would not call us very conservative at all. That is probably why there are now so very many of us. We are warning that today's liberal is threatening to denigrate the dignity of the individual and further erode our spiritual freedom and political liberty. We are no longer debating options within the parameters of the American system. We are, in fact, debating that very system itself.

"The conservative Republican value system instinctively identifies with the well-to-do, those successful achievers or inheritors of the free-enterprise society."

Conservative Values Lack Compassion

Paul Tsongas

Paul Tsongas served as the junior senator from Massachusetts before he was forced to abandon his political career because of cancer. As a promising young liberal in 1980, he gave the keynote address at the national convention of Americans for Democratic Action. In it he applauded the legacy of liberalism and stressed the need for liberals to develop a new agenda to solve current problems. In 1981 Tsongas elaborated on his speech in the book *The Road from Here*, an effort, the author stated, "to put my thesis into a coherent framework." In the viewpoint that follows, taken from that book, Tsongas presents a rationale for modern day liberals. He claims the values of liberals are more consistent with reality than are the values of conservatives.

As you read, consider the following questions:

1. What five values does the author say form the basis of the liberal tradition?
2. In the author's opinion, how do liberal values differ from conservative values?
3. Why does the author think conservative values are not consistent with American reality? Do you agree?

From THE ROAD FROM HERE: LIBERALISM AND REALITIES IN THE 1980's, by Paul Tsongas. Copyright © 1981 by Paul Tsongas. Reprinted by permission of Alfred A. Knopf, Inc.

Here I will suggest a framework of five values that can serve as a philosophical underpinning and that reflect the best of the liberal tradition.

Economic Justice. We must reject the economic exploitation of the individual. It is a grotesque fact of history that the "better" classes of society have been mainly responsible for such abuses. The slave trade was conducted by Europeans of learning, affluence, and culture. Slavery was accepted by those who wrote the Constitution and those who led the nation through its first seventy years. Child labor was aggressively employed by fathers who doted on their own children. Inadequate wages were imposed upon the immigrant masses by the great barons of industry. Areas of economic injustice exist today, but they cannot be tolerated. Resistance requires a sense of outrage, an unwillingness to accept exploitation as "the way it is," a capacity to "feel" a basic inequity.

Social Justice. We must deplore the social debasement of the individual. *All men are created equal*—these words may not recognize the reality of women, but they are of enormous consequence. The concept has become an expectation to be claimed and struggled for. It is not acceptable that men and women of any race, color, or religion should be forced to experience less than the full rights of citizenship.

Repudiate Discrimination

Political Justice. We must repudiate political discrimination against the individual. The idea of the consent of the governed spread from the American Revolution to other countries and became part of people's goals and expectations everywhere. Concepts such as self-determination, freedom of speech and assembly, no taxation without representation, universal suffrage, have for generations comprised the democratic ideal. Although authoritarian regimes exist in many nations, the principle of political justice is an established doctrine in the world community.

Respect for the Environment. We must protest the plunder of our resources in a manner out of harmony with the needs of our planet. The mechanized, urbanized, disposal lifestyle of modern industrial man clashes with the needs of the co-inhabitants of our earth, who have an equal right to survive. As steward of these resources, man must realize that the earth has a rhythm and a balance sheet, and they must be recognized on the earth's terms.

Concern for the Family of Man. We must repudiate the attitude of overlooking our values once we cross our national boundaries. The principles that we embrace at home—such as human rights— should not give way to expediency in our dealings with other nations. There needs to be a strong sense of brotherhood linking the various peoples of our world. The despair of the poor and helpless in other countries cannot be ignored. Only when we understand that there is a commonality linking all of us will we achieve a clear sense of what it means to be a part of the family of man.

Economic Justice

These values are commonly held by Americans in varying degrees. Indeed, the conservatives will argue that they also honor these values, but the true test is when and how they are applied.

To be specific, the preceding chapters began by seeking to ascertain the "reality" of any particular issue. That reality provides a frame of reference for action—i.e., the answer to the question of "what works?" Within the framework, however, is room either to employ or to reject the values referred to above.

Conservatism Is Based on Greed and Fear

To the question, "what conditions will generate growth and productivity?" conservatives have responded with a set of prescriptions premised upon the hypothetical power of human greed and fear. A society that simultaneously offers both the prospect of substantial wealth and the threat of severe poverty surely will inspire great feats of personal daring, dazzling entrepreneurialism, and cutthroat ambition. But just as surely it may reduce the capacity of its members to work together toward a common end. The conservative promise of prosperity is an ideology suited to a frontier economy in which risk-taking is apt to be more socially productive than cooperation, but it is hardly appropriate to an advanced industrial economy in which collaboration is critical. Liberalism must reestablish the connection between prosperity and social justice. In an advanced industrial economy like ours, and like those of our more productive neighbors, this is the only supply-side theory that makes lasting sense.

Robert Reich, *The New Republic*, February 21, 1981.

Let's take one of these values—economic justice—and apply it to a present-day reality—the energy crisis and the need for the decontrol of oil. Within the boundaries of that particular reality there is a great deal of room for policies that reflect this value, but only if we care to implement them.

Both major political parties endorse the idea of economic justice, but from different points of view. The conservative Republican value system instinctively identifies with the well-to-do, those successful achievers or inheritors of the free-enterprise society. The liberal Democratic value system instinctively identifies with the poor and the middle class—those with the least, or a lesser, capacity to adjust.

Decontrol—plus OPEC price increases—has two consequences: enormous oil company profits and higher energy charges to the consumer.

The conservative is not dismayed by these results; his constituency is well served by these profits and well insulated from rising prices. The liberal is troubled by these results because they violate his sense of values, his interpretation of what economic justice means. While he must accept the reality of decontrol, the liberal must argue for shock absorbers to cushion the impact on low- and middle-income citizens.

Government is supposed to act as a mechanism to protect those least able to protect themselves. Thus, the liberal supports a windfall-profits tax on oil-decontrol profits and would direct those funds to an energy assistance plan to ensure that no person freezes to death, to a conservation bank for low-interest loans to homeowners for weatherization, and to schemes to provide both mass transit and alternative sources of energy to reduce dependency on future oil price hikes. The goal of realism is thus served, but within a framework of economic justice that recognizes the problems of equity.

How different from the Reagan preference for decontrol without a windfall profits tax—and thus no mechanism to provide shock absorbers.

Political and Social Justice

Let's now consider an international reality, and apply to it the principles of political and social justice. The reality is the striving of the Third World for self-determination.

In the Republic of South Africa, the white man controls the country under the system of apartheid. He votes for his member of parliament, while the black lacks the vote and representation. The white can buy land anywhere in the country; the black is limited to acreage in barren, remote areas known as "black homelands." The white can work and live anywhere in Johannesburg or Capetown; the black who works there must leave the cities in the evening to sleep in segregated townships like Soweto. The white can eat anywhere, the black cannot. The white is free to travel, the black must carry a pass. There are laws against interracial marriage and separate public facilities for the races.

Apartheid is institutionalized racism—an anachronistic system with practices long since rejected in the United States. In America we have over the last 120 years attempted to change the racial status quo. It has not been an easy road, and there have been setbacks, but most of us are committed to this cause.

Now, given all this, the reality of Third World nationalism and the values of political and social justice would seem to provide a nice convergence of policy.

Nevertheless, how to deal with South Africa remains in dispute. The conservative sees a friendly regime in power. Ronald Reagan has said we should not turn our backs on those who have been allied with us in previous wars. (The fact that many Afrikaner leaders, including some eventual prime ministers, were openly pro-Nazi is conveniently overlooked.) From the conservative's East-West perspective, the pro-western stance of the South African government is the ruling value.

Liberal and Conservative Concepts of Freedom

Though the Founding Fathers believed in economic freedom, they realized that political freedom was the only obstacle to tyranny. Without it, the abuse of power, no matter what its nature, might go unchecked. But conservatives have reversed the order of priority. Demoting political freedom, they have elevated economic freedom to first place in the hierarchy of society's values.

Conservatives consider the freedom the right to go into business, to make profit, to spend and invest, to negotiate contracts, all without restriction. They recognize that to deter the unscrupulous, law must impose some regulation on these activities. Some concede the need for more regulation, some call for less. In their extreme form, conservatives conceive of freedom as the right to plunder. More often, they consider laws that go beyond simple police functions to be restrictions of freedom. Taxes, in this view, are threats to freedom. Social security, pure food and drug laws, farm production quotas, industrial safety standards are all impositions on freedom. Many consider labor unions to be in conflict with freedom. Government's role, according to the responsible conservative, is to encourage the maximum amount of economic freedom compatible with the preservation of society.

The liberal, on the other hand, considers freedom the right to speak, to write, to hold meetings, to form parties, to dissent from conventional opinion. Because he is committed to improving the lot of the distressed, he is a staunch defender of the means inherent within the Constitution for giving effect to new theories, innovations, social improvements. He is frequently irritated at the frustrations of constitutional government which permit conservatives to delay measures he considers overdue and defeat others that he deems essential. But he has learned that the mechanism for change does exist. This mechanism has its basis in political freedom.

Milton Viorst, *Liberalism: A Guide to Its Past, Present and Future in American Politics*, 1963. Reprinted with permission of the author.

Thus, while the conservative may embrace the values of political and social justice in theory, in practice they become secondary to his cold-warism, and thus expendable. (The same can be said for our current policy in El Salvador, and the myriad instances where the human rights banner has recently been lowered by the United States.) The liberal sees in South Africa the supremacy of those practices that have haunted America. Support of the South

African government amounts to de facto approval of apartheid, which is by definition a rejection of the values of political and social justice. The liberal, therefore, would employ the weight and influence of this nation to facilitate the coming of majority rule to South Africa and Namibia.

Respect for the Environment

Finally, let's take the value of respect for the environment, which is dismissed by very few. The reality here is the need for electricity. The conservative sees and approves plants fueled by nuclear power, coal, and natural gas. The liberal may see the same need, but only after conservation and renewables have been employed to the maximum extent.

The liberal insists upon an energy policy that provides the energy required, but with a minimized impact on the environment. While the conservative may respect the environment, he's not likely to go out of his way to alter energy policy to accommodate that consideration. These three examples reflect the underlying values that affect the lives of all us. And in all three cases I truly believe that the liberal values are more *consistent with the realities* than the conservative values. Insensitivity to the economic results of oil decontrol will lead to social unrest. Indifference to the impact of apartheid will eventually lead to violence and revolution. Obtuseness about the effect on the environment of fossil fuel consumption will lead to an all-too-rapid depletion of resources.

Liberal values are thus not only important in human terms, they are also functional. Indeed, the great leaps forward in this country have taken place when these values have broken through old norms. Above all, the values have worked. . . .

Conclusion

Liberalism has largely molded our present society. The elderly on social security and Medicare may forget that their grandparents had neither. Workers laboring in safe factories at decent wages may lose sight of the fact that their predecessors in the nineteenth century had neither. Young men finally stopped dying in Vietnam when liberal protests helped halt the war. Millions of children have been nurtured physically under the school lunch program and intellectually under Head Start. . . .

The conservatives in power today . . . have largely been absent, reluctant, or in opposition when the great issues of compassion were debated. An ideology linked to the wealthy and the entrepreneurial class (i.e., the 1981 Reagan tax cut) does not lend itself easily to serious concern about the poor or the blue-collar worker, the disadvantaged or the afflicted. It is altogether consistent for candidate Reagan to state that he would cut only "waste, fraud and abuse" from the federal budget and then, once in office, proceed to reduce or dismantle an entire range of human services. For conservatives, programs that provide economic and social assistance are simply not felt needs.

Given middle-class disenchantment in a time of economic strain, the demolition of programs aimed at the disadvantaged may seem good politics. But is it good government in a democratic society? Can you effectively run a system in which compassion is minimized by an administration whose inaugural was highlighted by the greatest coming together of mink coats, expensive jewelry, and private jets in Washington history?

There are too many bright young minds among the disadvantaged that will be wasted because necessary funds have gone to vested congressional interests through programs like tobacco subsidies. There are too many concerned citizens in the older cities who will be protesting the loss of industries because urban investment programs have been gutted while cost-ineffective water projects remain intact. There are too many average, non-ideological Americans who care about the quality of life, about clean air and water, about good education, about arts and culture, and about children whose intellectual progress is held back because of a lack of nutrition.

The conservative politician can't deal with such unfairness because he doesn't feel it. Those who live on the hill tend to wish that those in the valley below would just keep still. They forget that among the first Americans to regard themselves as victims of an unjust, uncaring, and unbending government were Paul Revere, George Washington, Benjamin Franklin, Thomas Jefferson, John Adams, Patrick Henry, and Alexander Hamilton.

Distinguishing Between Fact and Opinion

This activity is designed to help develop the basic reading and thinking skill of distinguishing between fact and opinion. Consider the following statement as an example: If a conservative, religious leader is elected president of the United States at some future date, that would be a fact. However, whether or not the United States would be better off socially, economically, politically, and even religiously with a conservative, religious president is a matter of opinion. Future historians would agree that the individual in question was a president of the United States. But their interpretations of the impact of his or her presidency probably would vary greatly.

When investigating controversial issues it is important that one be able to distinguish between statements of fact and statements of opinion.

Many of the following statements are taken from the viewpoints in this book. Some have other origins. Consider each statement carefully. *Mark O for any statement you believe is an opinion or interpretation of facts. Mark F for any statement you believe is a fact.*

If you are doing this activity as a member of a class or group, compare your answers with those of other class or group members. Be able to defend your answers. You may discover that others will come to different conclusions than you. Listening to the reasons others present for their answers may give you valuable insights in distinguishing between fact and opinion.

If you are reading this book alone, ask others if they agree with your answers. You too will find this interaction very valuable.

O = opinion
F = fact

1. In the 1960s, liberals were raising the important issues and working toward practical solutions.

2. There will be a desperate and crying need for the values of conservatism in the 1990s.

3. Conservatives generally believe that there exists a transcendent moral order, to which we ought to try to conform the ways of society.

4. One of the fundamental traits of the conservative attitude is a fear of change.

5. Conservatives are inclined to use the powers of government to prevent change or to limit its rate to whatever appeals to the more timid mind.

6. The typical conservative is usually a person of very strong moral convictions.

7. Conservatism fears new ideas because it has no distinctive principles of its own to oppose them.

8. The contest between liberals and conservatives is a moral battle.

9. Conservatives look to values and absolutes to direct them.

10. Welfarism has created a psychology of dependency. Instead of helping people to escape from poverty, tragically welfarism has created for millions a psychological ghetto of defeatism.

11. Generally speaking, conservatives tend to support big business while liberals tend to support labor.

12. Politically and economically, the United States is moving toward a socialistic, welfare state.

13. The conservatives in power today have largely been absent, reluctant, or in opposition when the great issues of compassion were debated.

14. The Democratic Party is now controlled by people who seem to be still living in the 1930s.

5

VIEWPOINT

"Conservative 'think tanks' . . . represent our best hope for arresting the momentum of the socialist mentality."

Conservative 'Think Tanks' Are America's Best Hope

Martin Stone

Martin Stone is a founding editor of *California Business* magazine and is its current president and board chairman. He writes a column called "Commentary" in the magazine, in which he speaks out on social and economic issues. The following viewpoint, which originally appeared in Stone's column, claims that current intellectual ferment is coming from the conservative side of the political spectrum. Although Stone resists being labeled as either a conservative or liberal, he suggests that all freedom-lovers join ranks with conservative organizations to fight the growing power and influence of government.

As you read, consider the following questions:

1. Why does the author think the American political left has no answers for the country's problems?
2. Why is he also disappointed with the political right and the Reagan Presidency?
3. Why does he believe conservative "think tanks" offer America its best hope for the future?

Martin Stone, "Who Will Save Us From the Worn-Out Liberals and the Misguided Conservatives?" *California Business*, June 1984. Reprinted with permission.

178

Since the early 1930s, most of the intellectual ferment on the American political scene has been on the left side of the political spectrum. Out of all this ferment came a dramatic shift from traditional American laissez-faire capitalistic economics to a blend of what I would call social welfare capitalism. The products of this change went by such names as The New Deal, The Fair Deal, The New Society, The Great Society and The War on Poverty. A massive expansion of federal government activities was involved, as well as an equivalent intrusion by the federal government into the affairs of individual citizens. Individual rights and liberties were compromised in order to promote the so-called overall social good.

The Role of Government Intervention

In my judgment, some of this government activity was justified on the grounds that technical and social evolution made necessary new sets of rule by which to define the relationship between individuals and the state. I have little doubt, for example, that without federal government intervention, the civil rights of minority citizens would not nearly approach the present-day level—which still contains significant degrees of injustice.

Furthermore, as long as our traditions and our regulations caused us to regard air, water and earth as free resources, to be used without a regard to long-term social impact, environmental degradation was bound to accelerate. Industry was actually encouraged to pump its gaseous wastes into the atmosphere, to dump its liquid wastes into bodies of water, and to dump its solid wastes into the most convenient land area. The individuals and industries polluting our environment in this manner actually benefited economically from doing so. The situation mandated a new set of laws to either prevent such degradation or to impose a direct cost upon the polluting activities.

In a number of other areas, too, government intervention was required in order to deal with changing conditions in society. But, as with most everything in life, the pendulum of change did not stop at the appropriate point of equilibrium. Instead, it carried the new direction to an unwarranted extreme, which in itself poses a threat to our society.

In my judgment, government intervention is a major threat to individual freedom in the United States today. It is a threat to our economic well-being and to our very survival. Furthermore, both of our major political parties share the responsibility for this threat.

The Political Left's Outdated View

The Democratic Party is now controlled by people who seem to be still living in the '30s. It is hostile to those who have built their prosperity through hard work and sacrifice; it treats the most successful members of our society as undesirables and seeks ways to bring them down to some level perceived as the acceptable norm. It views business as "bad," labor as "good," and economic equality rather than equality of opportunity as the desired force of government policy. . . .

In essence, neither Mondale, Gary Hart nor Jesse Jackson actually understands the American free enterprise system of economics; or, if they do, they don't believe in it. If they truly understood the system, how could they continually talk about tax deductions and credits—which enable people *to keep more of their own money*—as subsidies? The candidates' language convinces me they actually believe that we, as individuals, are servants of the state and that the product of our labor properly belongs to the state—except for whatever portion the state, in its wisdom, elects to permit us to keep. . . .

Leading Democratic candidates believe in the superior wisdom and benevolence of the government. This is evident in their advocacy of national industrial policies, wage and price controls, "tax-based incomes" policies, income redistribution ideas, etc.

The Disappointment of the Reagan Right

What I see on the right side of the political spectrum gives me no more comfort than my vision of the left. Ronald Reagan is the

Reprinted by permission: Tribune Media Services.

clearest representative of the ideology of the right to hold office in the United States in my lifetime. As a candidate and a political communicator, he espoused many ideas and attitudes with which I was sympathetic: the concept of limited government, balanced budgets, reduction of excess taxation on the most productive members of our society, elimination or reduction of welfare abuses—both business and social—and, above all, a dramatic reduction in the size and impact of the federal government. But what in fact has he done while serving as president?

(1) He proposed the most stringent government secrecy regulations in history. Without access to inside government information, it is impractical for citizens to protect themselves against government or to change improper policies or procedures. A democratic society can only survive as long as we have an informed and politically active citizenry.

(2) Because of his fear of the Russians, Reagan is attempting to turn the United States into a garrison state in which our resources and our individual liberties and rights are sacrificed to the need to cope with the "Soviet threat." This despite the fact that, almost unanimously, his own military chiefs of staff and former chiefs of staff, as well as virtually every past secretary of defense, state unequivocally that they would not trade our military strength for that of the Soviets. An insane escalation of the arms race threatens our survival, weakening us for the long-term economic struggle with the Soviets that will ultimately prove to be paramount in our international competition with them.

(3) Reagan, who is one of the leaders of the fight for a constitutional amendment mandating a balanced budget, has given us the worst fiscal deficits in our history and promises little relief from such deficits.

On the business welfare side of the equation, Reagan's record is abysmal. His administration, although talking anti-farm subsidy rhetoric, has increased the level of farm subsidies more than at any time in the past 30 years. Annual U.S. farm subsidies now total more than $20 billion. When Reagan took office, farm subsidies totaled approximately $3 billion a year.

Reagan's administration has been extraordinarily sensitive to the demands of business. We businessmen have been in the front of the line with our hands out, pressuring for special favors. If we look around, we see that we are in the process of protecting the auto companies and the steel companies, bailing out the banks and savings and loans, and, in a myriad of ways, protecting American capitalists from the risks of loss. A healthy free enterprise economy mandates that weak companies, or companies that overextend themselves, should perish and their resources be transferred to the use of vital, energetic, growing companies and industries. We must reduce the level of our intervention in business affairs. The government's role should be neutral in terms of its impact on free market competition.

If we business people, who are at the core of the American free enterprise system of competition, erode it whenever doing so will gain us temporary economic benefit, how can we expect to rally public opposition against the socialistic policies of those who would do away with our system of free market competitive economics?

Conservative Think Tanks Are America's Best Hope

At the beginning of this article, I mentioned that for most of the past 50 years, most political intellectual ferment had come from the left. That is no longer the case. The one great hopeful sign I see is that new intellectual ferment is coming from the conservative side of the political spectrum. Conservative "think tanks" such as the Cato Institution, the Council for a Competitive Economy and the Pacific Institute are producing extraordinary work designed to lay the intellectual foundation for the rolling back of government intervention and domination of our individual and business lives. These organizations are still small, but their influence in universities has been large and their lobbying has been effective in Congress at times. In my judgment, they represent our best hope for arresting the momentum of the socialistic mentality that has begun to dominate our political levers of power.

These conservative organizations have helped develop the intellectual foundation for the private contracting of public services, a concept that has shown itself capable of bringing about enormous reductions of government costs. They have been in the forefront of the fight to deregulate the transportation and banking industries. They have done the best job of research and analysis on the problems of our Social Security and Medicaid systems. They have been in the forefront of the fight to break the education bureaucracy's stranglehold on the education of our children.

These organizations deserve the support of business people and believers in individual liberty. But make no mistake about it, they are not friends of special favors for business. They oppose import quotas, federal marketing orders that restrict production of farm products, subsidized cost loans to exporters and bailouts of failing businesses.

Open business competition is tough and demanding, and some of our business activities will be harmed if we have to compete openly and without special favor. If we, as business people, truly believe in our system, we can't support it only when there is not sacrifice demanded of us, and we can't continually seek favors from a government we hope to diminish in size and impact. Furthermore, individuals who are not in business but who truly believe in individual liberty have got to join with enlightened business interests in this fight against the encroachment of government into our lives.

"It is time that the center-left articulated its own response. . . . Substantial resources and groups are available to create a prospective center-left coalition."

Liberals Must Counter Conservative 'Think Tanks'

John S. Saloma III

John S. Saloma III was the first president of the liberal Republican Ripon Society. A Harvard Ph.D., he taught political science at M.I.T. and served as a staff associate at the John F. Kennedy Institute of Politics at Harvard. Shortly before his death in 1983, the author finished a manuscript titled *Ominous Politics: The New Conservative Labyrinth*, a book that traces the development of the conservative movement of the past three decades. In the viewpoint that follows, the author presents an agenda for liberals to follow to counteract the efforts of the conservative movement.

As you read, consider the following questions:

1. To what does the author refer with the term "contextual politics," and why does he see it as a danger to liberal principles?
2. Before outlining the basis of his recommended center-left coalition, what positive aspects of the conservative movement does Mr. Saloma identify?

The thesis of *Ominous Politics* is simple but dramatic: Over a period of more than two decades, political conservatives have quietly built a vast coalition of think tanks, political action groups, religious broadcasters, corporate political organizations, senators and representatives, Republican Party officials, and other groups with budgets totaling hundreds of millions of dollars annually. I emphasize the word "quietly" because this major development in American politics has not been much discussed in the media, or been the subject of serious study and publication. It has arrived almost unannounced.

Conservatives have largely succeeded in building institutions that incorporate a new long-term strategic dimension into American politics. The high level of organizational development has given political conservatism a decisive advantage over poorly organized liberals in the 1980s. It is impossible to know how events will unfold, but the title of my book, *Ominous Politics*, represents my concern. . . .

Think Tanks Influence Public Opinion

The conservative think tanks are the most impressive evidence of strategic planning by the conservatives. . . .

Think tanks are shaping the attitudes of American voters and altering the context in which they consider issues. What they do can best be described as contextual politics. AEI's *Public Opinion* magazine and Center for Research in Advertising, the Republican National Committee consulting group on "the new rhetoric," and the public-relations campaigns of the conservative think tanks in general, have all contributed here.

Contextual politics is a brilliant and disturbing innovation because it falls outside our traditional definition of politics. Institutional advertising, designed to influence political opinion, is not completely new to American politics—conservatives used it as long ago as the last Senate campaign of Robert Taft in Ohio. What is new is the scale and sophistication. Take, for example, the campaign in California to defeat Proposition 5, the antismoking initiative, in 1978. Californians for Common Sense, the "No on 5" committee funded by a consortium of tobacco companies headed by R.J. Reynolds, spent a record $6 million to defeat the initiative. Campaign literature featured a patriot, the Liberty Bell (also the logo of the Heritage Foundation), and a scroll headed WE THE PEOPLE. Billboards and radio spots asked, "What will the regulators do next?" The underlying antiregulation message prepared voters for a whole range of issues beyond the immediate campaign.

Conservatives have appropriated powerful words and symbols—freedom, family, work, religion, common sense, patriotism—in a way that has caught the liberals unaware. Norman Lear's 1982 television special *I Love Liberty* may be the first evidence that the liberals are prepared to contest this terrain. Conservative media campaigns on issues like the Soviet arms buildup and government spending and inflation are also attempts to condition American public opinion. The think tanks provide a core of fact and the aura of respectability to these efforts.

In all these ways, conservative think tanks pursue activist agendas well beyond policy research as it has been traditionally defined or practiced by liberal think tanks. Every indication since the Reagan election is that these institutions are still growing. They are obviously a long-term investment that the conservatives expect to yield substantial returns through the 1980s into the 1990s. . . .

It is my contention that the liberals' focus is too limited. Their failure to place the New Right in historical context has led them to underestimate the conservative challenge. There are at least two deficiencies in much liberal analysis of the New Right. First, many liberals fail to perceive the interconnections among the New Right, the old right, and Republican Party organizations. Second, and more important, they fail to see the mutually supportive roles of the conservative political action groups, think tanks, and other sectors like the corporate community. . . .

The steady development of numerous conservative political action groups, and the growth of the conservative think tanks, represents something quite new—in available resources and sophistication—in American politics. Add to this the ideological fervor of the conservative activists and there is a formidable force for change. The strident anti-Communism of the Sharon statement ("The forces of International Communism are, at present, the greatest single threat to those liberties" and "The United States should stress victory over, rather than coexistence with, this menace") survives in conservative/neoconservative pressures on Reagan to terminate the West European-Soviet gas pipeline, intervene militarily in Central America, and in the 1983 Miami speech in which Reagan called the Soviet Union the focus of all evil in the world. On economic and social policy issues, younger conservatives are equally determined. "We are different from previous generations of conservatives," says Paul Weyrich. "We are no longer working to preserve the status quo. We are radicals, working to overturn the present power structure of this country." . . .

The Center-Left Must Develop a Strategy

What happens in the next few years depends in part on unpredictable developments tied to the word "economy." The weak recovery may be followed by another downturn, with unforeseen political consequences. The continuing budgetary crisis may precipitate a constitutional convention calling for extensive changes in the structure of government, a possibility the conser-

185

vatives have both encouraged and prepared for. But in any scenario, one thing is clear: the institutions of the conservative network will help shape post-Reagan America.

How to respond is a question that the political center and left have barely begun to address. I use the term "center-left" to emphasize the importance of contesting the political center. The conservatives have been able to accommodate differences on the right and extend their coalition to the center. The center-left has much further to go in developing a common strategy.

Don Wright, *Miami News*. Reprinted with permission.

We can acknowledge and support certain highly positive aspects of conservatism. First, the conservatives have made a substantial investment in the future of the American political system. The building of the network is itself a major accomplishment. Second, the conservatives and the business community have to their credit introduced a useful perspective into American politics and public policy. They show concern for the health of the economy, dealing with the welfare state, and achieving fiscal balance. Finally, there are legitimate national security, defense, and intelligence problems being addressed by the conservatives at the international level. We should view conservatism as basically constructive in impulse. While we may not share its vision of America, conservatism is committed as much to building the new as to replacing the old.

One appropriate response, then, is selective support, acknowledgeing and endorsing those reforms that, to use a favorite conservative term, make "common sense."

Describing the labyrinth helps to identify it in the public mind, but that is not sufficient. It must be brought under public scrutiny and held accountable for the exercise of its power if it is to be accepted as part of the democratic process. Only an effective opposition can exercise this responsibility. The media can play a constructive role, especially through investigative reporting, but political opposition is more appropriately exercised by people in politics. Ultimately, only a stance that transcends both liberal and conservative positions can resolve the apparently fundamental differences that now separate us.

In the early months of the Reagan Administration, Richard Viguerie predicted that "the next few years will see a massive battle of conservatives and liberals to determine who governs the nation for the next three decades—and we've got a head start of years on them." Events indeed seem to be moving in the conservative direction, producing a dangerous imbalance in the political system. They have outthought and outplanned the liberals. It may well take the center-left the rest of the decade to restore the balance.

Liberals have reacted to the Reagan Administration by organizing a number of political action groups, think tanks, and publications. The response of Democrats in Congress, however, is essentially tactical and risks appearing negative and narrowly partisan. The leaders of the liberal coalition of past decades are growing older and are unlikely to spearhead a liberal counteroffensive. And a distressing number of younger liberal politicians are so-called neoliberals who seem all too willing to adopt the rhetoric of the conservatives—which means accepting conservative definitions of what the problems are.

A New Center-Left Coalition Is Needed

It is time that the center-left articulated its own response. The developments I have described require a response that goes beyond traditional Democratic Party politics. Substantial resources and groups are available to create a prospective center-left coalition. They include:

- the core institutions of the old liberal-labor-civil-rights coalition, including the generation of leaders that developed in the 1960s and 1970s

- the liberal intelligentsia in the universities and major urban centers, who should be able to counterbalance at least partially the financial resource advantages of the conservatives through intelligent action, i.e., working "smart"

- the moral legacy of the civil-rights movement and the powerful ideal of a multiracial society that advances social justice

187

and unifies rather than divides American society

- the women's movement, perhaps the most significant political force of the last third of this century—effectively excluded from Reagan conservatism

- moderate and liberal Republicans in the Congress, strategic industrial states, and the business and professional communities

- allies within the corporate power structure who would assume more social responsibility than is represented by Friedmanism or neoconservatism

- a new socially humane, post-Keynesian economics of the center-left that addresses the realities of American capitalism, including its economic power

- the public demand for a sensible arms control and disarmament strategy, exemplified by the widespread, spontaneous support for a nuclear freeze

- the great, largely unorganized constituency for the defense of the Constitution and constitutional values against radical political change

- the leaders of and participants in the other political movements that came of age in the 1960s and 1970s—the anti-Vietnam War movement, the consumer and environmental movements, the racial and sexual minorities, the elderly, the handicapped, and so on

- the cultural alternative force represented by the "counter culture" and youth movements of the 1960s and since—including the human potential/consciousness movement and New Age politics

- global citizen "networking" and organization that transcends the nationalist, militarist focus of the conservative movement and the elite character of its current international contacts

- the widespread support for an American foreign policy that advances democratic values and social justice, most noticeably in Latin America, where reform elements in the Roman Catholic Church have made an unusual public stand

- the potential for participatory, interactive democratic politics presented by information technology and communications media; cable television, personal computer networking, satellite relays, and so on (the telephone still provides one of the most powerful tools and models for democratic politics)

- the commitment of the overwhelming majority of professionals in the communications media to the values of democratic as opposed to a technocratic, manipulative politics

• financial resources that include both traditional sources (wealthy contributors, labor unions, liberal foundations, some corporations) and the affluent, socially committed young professionals of the middle class

Putting together a coalition of the center-left is a formidable task for the political generation trained and tested in the 1960s and 1970s. Yet, only as we learn to put aside internal disagreements and differences in goals and function together as worthy opponents to the conservatives will we earn the opportunity to lead America to the realization of a broader vision.

"Most neoconservatives believe that the last, best hope of humanity at this time is an intellectually and morally reinvigorated liberal capitalism."

The Case for Neoconservatism

Irving Kristol

Irving Kristol is Professor of Social Thought at New York University's Graduate School of Business Administration, co-editor of *The Public Interest*, and a member of the board of contributors of the *Wall Street Journal*. A political radical when he graduated from City College in 1940, Kristol claims he has been moving steadily to the right since 1942. He has journeyed from liberalism to conservatism and is now the principle spokesman for neoconservatism. In the viewpoint that follows, he outlines what he considers to be the basic tenets of neoconservatism.

As you read, consider the following questions:

1. In the author's opinion, how did the neoconservative movement begin, and how did the term "neoconservative" originate?
2. How does neoconservatism differ from conservatism?
3. After reading this viewpoint, why do you think neoconservatism is so difficult to categorize, and what do you predict for the movement's future?

Irving Kristol, "Confessions of a True, Self-Confessed—Perhaps the Only—Neoconservative," *Public Opinion*, October/November 1979. Copyright 1979 by the American Enterprise Institute. Reprinted with permission.

It has long been a cliché of liberal discourse that what this country needs is a truly intelligent and sophisticated conservatism to replace the rather primitive, philistine, and often racist conservatism that our history is only too familiar with. This new and desirable conservatism should have a philosophic and literary dimension which would rectify the occasional excesses of liberal ideology. It should even have a nebulous but definitely genteel political dimension, since it is likely that we shall always, at interval, need a brief interregnum of conservative government whose function it is to consolidate and ratify liberal reforms. The ideal conservative president, from this liberal point of view, would be a Dwight Eisenhower who read Lionel Trilling instead of paperback Westerns, who listened to chamber music instead of playing golf—but who would be, in all other respects, as inert as the real President Eisenhower in fact was.

What we absolutely do *not* need or want, from this liberal perspective, is a conservatism with strong ideas of its own about economic policy, social policy, or foreign policy—especially if these ideas can pass academic muster and survive intellectual debate. Such a conservatism might actually affect public policy, even become a shaping force in American politics, and this is simply impermissible. The very possibility of such a conservatism is a specter that haunts the liberal imagination and can propel it into frenzies of exorcism.

The Origin of the Term 'Neoconservative'

It is because the liberal intellectual community—and particularly the liberal-Left intellectual community, which is not quite the same thing, if almost the same thing—sees "neoconservatism" as representing such an awful possibility that it is so terribly agitated about it. Note: It is *they*, not us, who are excited. It is even they who gave us our name in the first place (specifically, it was Michael Harrington). *We* don't go around talking about neoconservatism. Indeed, such supposed representatives of this "movement" as Daniel Bell, Daniel Patrick Moynihan, Nathan Glazer, Norman Podhoretz, Aaron Wildavsky, Samuel Huntington, Roger Starr, Seymour Martin Lipset, and James Q. Wilson all shy away from the designation—some of them quite violently. Others, such as Robert Nisbet and Edward Banfield, call themselves "conservatives," without benefit of qualification. I myself have accepted the term, perhaps because, having been named Irving, I am relatively indifferent to baptismal caprice. But I may be the only living and self-confessed neoconservative, at large or in captivity.

It was to be expected, therefore, that the first book on neoconservatism would be written by one of *them*, not by one of *us*. Peter Steinfels is a Left-liberal journalist, a "democratic socialist" apparently, and his book, *The Neoconservatives: The Men Who Are Changing America's Politics*, is a polemic disguised as a report and

A Description of Neoconservatism

1. Neo-conservatism is not at all hostile to the idea of a welfare state, but it is critical of the Great Society version of this welfare state. In general, it approves of those social reforms that, while providing needed security and comfort to the individual in our dynamic, urbanized society, do so with a minimum of bureaucratic intrusion in the individual's affairs. Such reforms would include, of course, social security, unemployment insurance, some form of national health insurance, some kind of family-assistance plan, etc. In contrast, it is skeptical of those social programs that create vast and energetic bureaucracies to "solve social problems." In short, while being for the welfare state, it is opposed to the paternalistic state. It also believes that this welfare state will best promote the common good if it is conceived in such a way as not to go bankrupt.

2. Neo-conservatism has great respect—it is fair to say it has learned to have great respect—for the power of the market to respond efficiently to economic realities while preserving the maximum degree of individual freedom. Though willing to interfere with the market for overriding social purposes, it prefers to do so by "rigging" the market, or even creating new markets, rather than by direct bureaucratic controls. Thus it is more likely to favor housing vouchers for the poor than government-built low-income projects.

3. Neo-conservatism tends to be respectful of traditional values and institutions: religion, the family, the "high culture" of Western civilization. If there is any one thing that neo-conservatives are unanimous about, it is their dislike of the "counter-culture" that has played so remarkable a role in American life over these past fifteen years. Neo-conservatives are well aware that traditional values and institutions do change in time, but they prefer that such

---

"fair" commentary. The pretense is even more annoying than the polemic, which takes the form of interspersing summaries of our presumed views with constant reminders—lest the reader be contaminated—of just how far short these fall from wholesome "progressive" opinion. (There is also the insinuation that neoconservatism is really a profit-making enterprise disguised as intellectual work.) This rhetorical strategy makes for a long but tedious book, the reading of which is a wearying experience. It is as if Mr. Steinfels, morally opposed to capital punishment, had decided to nag neoconservatism to death.

I do not wish to suggest that the book is without merit. There is, for instance, an excellent couple of sentences on page 4:

> Political thought—in the United States today—is moving steadily in two directions. There are those, like democratic socialists, who feel they must reach beyond contemporary liberalism in order to fulfill its promises. And there are those, like the

change be gradual and organic. They believe that the individual who is abruptly "liberated" from the sovereignty of traditional values will soon find himself experiencing the vertigo and despair of nihilism. Nor do they put much credence in the notion that individuals can "create" their own values and then incorporate them into a satisfying "life-style." Values emerge out of the experience of generations and represent the accumulated wisdom of these generations; they simply cannot be got out of rap sessions about "identity" or "authenticity."

4. Neo-conservatism affirms the traditional American idea of equality, but rejects egalitarianism—the equality of condition for all citizens—as a proper goal for government to pursue. The equality proclaimed by the Declaration of Independence is an equality of natural rights—including the right to become unequal (within limits) in wealth, or public esteem, or influence. Without *that* right, equality becomes the enemy of liberty. To put it in more homely terms: the encouragement of equality of opportunity is always a proper concern of democratic government. But it is a dangerous sophistry to insist that there is no true equality of opportunity unless and until everyone ends up with equal shares of everything.

5. In foreign policy, neo-conservatism believes that American democracy is not likely to survive for long in a world that is overwhelmingly hostile to American values, if only because our transactions (economic and diplomatic) with foreign nations are bound eventually to have a profound impact on our own domestic economic and political system. So neo-conservatives are critical of the post-Vietnam isolationism now so popular in Congress, and many are suspicious of "detente" as well.

Irving Kristol, *Newsweek*, January 19, 1976. Copyright © 1976, by Newsweek, Inc. All Rights Reserved. Reprinted by permission.

neoconservatives, who feel they must reach beyond contemporary liberalism to preserve its heritage.

That is very well put—though it would be more correct to talk not of the promises *of* liberalism, but of the promises generated *by* and grafted *onto* liberalism in the course of this century. Democratic socialism can be seen as the fulfillment of liberalism only in a Hegelian sense—that is, it absorbs, transcends, and nullifies it, all at the same time. Neoconservatism, on the other hand, is indeed "reformationist" as Mr. Steinfels suggests. It tries to "reach beyond" contemporary liberalism in the way that all reformations, religious or political, do—by a return to the original sources of liberal vision and liberal energy so as to correct the warped version of liberalism that is today's orthodoxy.

Another way of defining these two antithetical tendencies is to say that the one is modern-utopian, the other classical-realist in temper and intellectual inclination. Nothing reveals this more clearly than Mr. Steinfels's accusation against neoconservatism that it is committed to "stability as the prerequisite for justice rather than the other way around." I do not know of a single political philosopher, from Plato to Tocqueville, or any of the founding fathers (always excepting an occasional wayward remark by Jefferson), who would have thought such a commitment anything but obviously sensible. To demand "justice" as a precondition for political stability is to make a demand on this world which the world has ever refused to concede. Mr. Steinfels, who is a Catholic intellectual—he is executive editor of *Commonweal*—has, in his passion for "justice now," forgotten everything he may once have learned from reading St. Augustine or St. Thomas.

Neoconservatism's Distinctive Features

It should be clear by now that I do think there really is such a thing as neoconservatism—but it is most misleading to think of it as any kind of "movement." It holds no meetings, has no organizational form, has no specific programmatic goals, and when two neoconservatives meet they are more likely to argue with one another than to confer or conspire. But it is there, nevertheless—an impulse that ripples through the intellectual world; a "persuasion," to use a nice old-fashioned term; a mode of thought (but not quite a school of thought).

What are its distinctive features? I shall list them as I see them—but to say that this listing is unofficial would be the understatement of the decade.

1. Neoconservatism is a current of thought emerging out of the academic-intellectual world and provoked by disillusionment with contemporary liberalism. Its relation to the business community—the traditional source of American conservatism—is loose and uneasy, though not necessarily unfriendly.

2. Unlike previous such currents of thought—for example, the Southern Agrarians or the Transcendentalists of the nineteenth century—neoconservatism is antiromantic in substance and temperament. Indeed, it regards political romanticism—and its twin, political utopianism—of any kind as one of the plagues of our age. This is but another way of saying it is a philosophical-political impulse rather than a literary-political impulse. Or, to put it still another way: Its approach to the world is more "rabbinic" than "prophetic."

3. The philosophical roots of neoconservatism are to be found mainly in classical—that is, premodern, preideological—political philosophy. Here the teaching and writing of the late Leo Strauss (never mentioned by Mr. Steinfels) are of importance, though many neoconservatives find him somewhat too wary of modernity. Neoconservatives are admiring of Aristotle, respectful of Locke, distrustful of Rousseau.

4. The attitude of neoconservatives to bourgeois society and the

bourgeois ethos is one of detached attachment. In the spirit of Tocqueville, neoconservatives do not think that liberal-democratic capitalism is the best of all imaginable worlds—only the best, under the circumstances, of all possible worlds. This *modest* enthusiasm distinguishes neoconservatism from the Old Right and the New Right—both of which are exceedingly suspicious of it.

5. Neoconservatism is inclined to the belief that a predominantly market economy—just how "predominant" is a matter for some disagreement—is a necessary if not sufficient precondition for a liberal society. (Daniel Bell, as the theoretician for what may be called our "social-democratic wing," would presumably take issue with this judgment.) It also sees a market economy as favorable to economic growth.

Reprinted by permission: Tribune Media Services.

6. Neoconservatives believe in the importance of economic growth, not out of any enthusiam for the material goods of this world, but because they see economic growth as indispensable for social and political stability. It is the prospect of economic growth that has made it possible to think—against the grain of premodern political thought—of democracy as a viable and enduring sociopolitical system.

7. Neoconservatives, though respecting the market as an economic mechanism, are not libertarian in the sense, say, that

Milton Friedman and Friedrich A. von Hayek are. A conservative welfare state—what once was called a "social insurance" state—is perfectly consistent with the neoconservative perspective. So is a state that takes a degree of responsibility for helping to shape the preferences that the people exercise in a free market—to "elevate" them, if you will. Neoconservatives, moreover, believe that it is natural for people to *want* their preferences to be elevated. The current version of liberalism, which prescribes massive government intervention in the marketplace but an absolute laissez-faire attitude toward manners and morals, strikes neoconservatives as representing a bizarre inversion of priorities.

8. Neoconservatives look upon family and religion as indispensable pillars of a decent society. Indeed, they have a special fondness for all of those intermediate institutions of a liberal society which reconcile the need for community with the desire for liberty.

Conclusion

Karl Marx once wrote that the human race would eventually face the choice between socialism and barbarism. Well, we have seen enough of socialism in our time to realize that, in actuality as distinct from ideality, it can offer neither stability nor justice, and that in many of its versions it seems perfectly compatible with barbarism. So most neoconservatives believe that the last, best hope of humanity at this time is an intellectually and morally reinvigorated liberal capitalism.

I could go on but I had better not. I suspect that too many of my neoconservative friends will already have taken exception to one or another thing I have said. For this is an intellectual current full of all sorts of little knotty whirlpools, each being agitated by some problem in political, social, or economic theory that needs further exploration, further thought. And that, I think, is what makes neoconservatism so interesting—the fact that it is as concerned with the questions it cannot yet satisfactorily answer as with those it thinks contemporary liberalism has answered incorrectly.

Construct Your Own Political Spectrum Diagram

Viewpoint one in the book's first chapter presents an argument for the usefulness of diagraming the political spectrum. It presents a bipolar, straight-line continuum diagram. After reading other viewpoints in this book, particularly those in chapter one, you may not agree that the bipolar, straight-line continuum best represents political reality in contemporary America.

This exercise begins with the assumption that a diagram of the spectrum is a helpful tool in understanding the differences and relationships between America's competing political ideologies. Its purpose is to help you decide which diagram best represents America's political spectrum. Following are four alternative diagrams. Consider the strengths and weaknesses of each. You may want to include other models, not presented here, or you may want to create your own diagram. In considering the alternatives, answer each of the following questions:

1. How does each diagram distort or inadequately visualize some aspect of American political reality?
2. What is the greatest visual strength of each model?
3. What model do you think best represents America's political spectrum?

If you are doing this exercise as a member of a group or class, work in small groups of four to six. Compare your group's results with those of the other groups.

The Bipolar, Straight-line Continuum Model

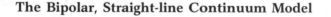

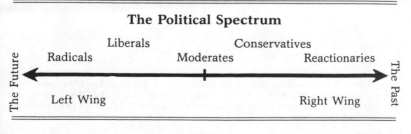

The Political Spectrum

197

The Maddox & Lilie Model

		Government Intervention in Economic Affairs	
		For	Against
Expansion of Personal Freedoms	For	Liberal	Libertarian
	Against	Populist	Conservative

The Libertarian Model

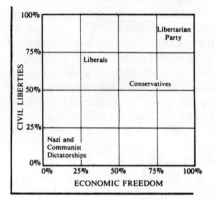

The Diamond Model

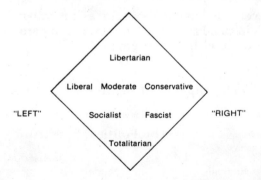

The Maddox & Lilie Model is taken from chapter one of this book. The Libertarian Model is taken from *The Political News*, a newspaper published by the Libertarian Party of Minnesota. The diamond model is taken from Ferdinand V. Solara, *Key Influences in the American Right*.

Periodical Bibliography

The following list of periodical articles deals with the subject matter of this chapter.

David M. Alpern — "The Right: A House Divided?" *Newsweek*, February 1, 1981.

Gregg Easterbrook — "Ideas Move Nations," *The Atlantic Monthly*, January 1986.

Milton Ellerin & Allisa H. Kesten — "The New Right: An Emerging Force on the Political Scene," *USA Today*, March 1981.

Esquire — "Neoconservatism: An Idea Whose Time Is Now," February 13, 1979.

George Gilder — "Ex-Neoconservative Praises the New Right for Commonsense Stands on the Issues," *Conservative Digest*, September 1980.

George Gilder — "Why I Am Not a Neoconservative," *National Review*, March 5, 1982.

Jeffrey Hart — "Gang Warfare in Chicago," *National Review*, June 6, 1986.

Jesse Helms — "Conservatism: 'Political Philosophy of the Day,'" *New Guard*, Spring 1981.

Charles R. Kesler — "The Reasonableness of Conservatism," *National Review*, December 31, 1980.

Russell Kirk — "Conservatism: A Succinct Description," *National Review*, September 3, 1982.

John Lukacs — "The American Conservatives," *Harpers*, January 1984.

Connaught Marshner — "Why Joseph Sobran Is Fighting for the American Family," *Conservative Digest*, May 1986.

Michael Novak — "Why I am Not a Conservative," *National Review*, June 26, 1981.

James Nuechterlein — "Neoconservatism & Irving Kristol," *Commentary*, August 1984.

John S. Saloma — "Old Right? New Right, *One* Right" *The Nation*, January 14, 1984.

Earl Shorris — "The Jews of the New Right," *The Nation*, May 8, 1982.

199

Fred Siegel — "Notes on the New Right," *Commonweal*, May 8, 1981.

Isidore Silver — "Neoconservatism vs. Conservatism," *Commonweal*, July 31, 1981.

Joseph Sobran — "Pensees: Notes for the Reactionary of Tomorrow," *National Review*, December 31, 1985.

Stephen J. Tonsor — "The Foundaton and the Academy," *National Review*, May 14, 1982.

U.S. News & World Report — "The Conservative Network: How It Plans to Keep on Winning," July 20, 1981.

Erik von Kuehnelt-Leddihn — "Is Ideology Useless?" *National Review*, June 10, 1983.

Erik von Kuehnelt-Leddihn — "The Portland Declaration," *National Review*, October 16, 1981.

David Wagner — "The New Right and the New Pluralism," *National Review*, May 23, 1986.

James Watt — "Liberals Chisel at the Three Pillars of Society," *U.S. News & World Report*, November 11, 1985.

Steven R. Weisman — "What Is a Conservative?" *The New York Times Magazine*, August 31, 1980.

George F. Will — "The Soul of Conservatism," *Newsweek*, November 11, 1985.

Annotated Book Bibliography

Walter T. Anderson, ed.
: *Rethinking Liberalism*. New York: Avon Books, 1983. Critical of "traditional liberalism," sixteen contributors suggest new liberal stances on a variety of issues.

Aristotle
: *The Politics*. Ernest Barker, tr., New York: Oxford University Press, 1946. Aristotle's analysis of the three major forms of government: monarchy, oligarchy, and democracy. The work examines the strengths and weaknesses of each and is predicated upon the author's opinion that humans are political animals who, by nature, function best in a political state.

David Boaz, ed.
: *Left, Right & Babyboom: America's New Politics*. Washington, DC: Cato Institute, 1986. Fifteen political analysts evaluate current trends on the American political scene and the impact of the babyboom generation on political parties and candidates.

William F. Buckley Jr., ed.
: *American Conservative Thought in the Twentieth Century*. Indianapolis: Bobbs—Merrill, 1970. Twenty-six conservatives, including the editor, analyze different aspects of conservatism.

William F. Buckley Jr.
: *Up from Liberalism*. Briarcliff Manor, NY: Stein & Day, 1985. Although it savages American liberalism as it existed three decades ago, it is a classic statement by the country's most famous conservative.

James Burnham
: *Suicide of the West: An Essay on the Meaning and Destiny of Liberalism*. Lake Bluff, IL: Regnery Gateway, 1985. A thorough and critical analysis of liberalism, claiming the pervasive acceptance of liberalism is an obstacle to the survival of western civilization. It is provocative, comprehensive and presents a conservative's perspective of liberalism's influence.

Lewis A. Coser & Irving Howe, eds.
: *The New Conservatives: A Critique from the Left*. New York: Quadrangle, 1974. Essays of left wing criticism, claiming neoconservatives are attempting to bring

about a counterrevolution of declining
expectations in a liberal country with a
history of liberal successes.

John Patrick Diggins	*The Lost Soul of American Politics: Virtue, Self-Interest, and the Foundations of Liberalism*. Basic Books, 1984. Difficult to read, it investigates the marriage of American liberalism's self-interest and Calvinism's public sacrifice. It laments the loss, or at least current absence, of a political morality or cultural virtue in American political theory and practice.
Kenneth M. Dolbeare & Patricia Dolbeare	*American Ideologies*. Boston: Houghton Mifflin, 1976. Although dated, the chapters on liberalism and conservatism provide good, easy-to-read descriptions.
William Gerber	*American Liberalism: Laudable End, Controversial Means*. Boston: Twayne Publishers, 1975. An excellent overview of the foundations, history and meaning of liberalism, emphasizing American liberalism. Includes valuable footnoting and a comprehensive bibliography.
Barry Goldwater	*The Conscience of a Conservative*. New York: Hillman Books, 1960. A conservative program and philosophy, written to deal with the issues of its time.
Robert A. Goldwin, ed.	*Left, Right and Center: Essays on Liberalism and Conservatism in the United States*. Chicago: Rand McNally & Company, 1967. Presents not only arguments by liberals and conservatives, but statements by spokesmen who are critical of both isms.
William R. Harbour	*The Foundations of Conservative Thought*. Notre Dame: University of Notre Dame Press, 1982. Introduction has a helpful ten point definition of conservatism from a religious view, and it has an appendix of short biographical sketches of prominent conservatives.
Louis Hartz	*The Liberal Tradition in American Politics*. New York: Harcourt, Brace & Jovanovich, 1962. Claims America's political philosophy is liberalism, based on the theories of John Locke.
Hubert H. Humphrey	*The Cause Is Mankind*. New York: Frederick A. Praeger, 1964. An argument for liberalism by an optimistic advocate.

Willmoore Kendall   *The Conservative Affirmation*. New York: Henry Regnery Company, 1985. Identifies American conservatism in general and its relationship to basic issues.

Russell Kirk, ed.   *The Portable Conservative Reader*. New York: Penquin Books, 1982. A comprehensive anthology of conservative statements from Edmund Burke to Irving Kristol.

Irving Kristol   *Reflections of a Neoconservative*. New York: Basic Books, 1983. The father of neoconservatism describes his evolution from socialism to neoconservatism.

Michael Kronenwetter   *Are You a Liberal? Are You a Conservative?* New York: Franklin Watts, 1984. Short, easy-to-read look at the historical development of liberalism and conservatism with emphasis on the current American scene.

Eugene McCarthy   *A Liberal Answer to the Conservative Challenge*. New York: Macfadden Books, 1964. An argument for liberalism in the 1960s, contrasting its methods and principles to conservatism's in an issue by issue comparison.

Noccolo Machiavelli   *The Prince*. Robert M. Adams, ed. and tr., New York: W.W. Norton, 1977. The classic work which ushered in the modern era of political philosophy. The excellent translation clearly voices Machiavelli's view that the purpose of political leadership should be the acquisition and maintenance of power.

Douglas MacLean & Claudia Mills, eds.   *Liberalism Reconsidered*. Totowa, NJ: Rowman & Allenheld, 1983. Essays analyzing the contemporary meaning of the term "liberalism" as a philosophical theory.

William S. Maddox & Stuart A. Lilie   *Beyond Liberal and Conservative: Reassessing the Political Spectrum*. Washington, DC: Cato Institute, 1984. The authors go beyond the traditional liberal-conservative view of the political spectrum, by separating questions of economic policy from issues involving civil liberties. They claim America has four basic ideological groups: liberals, conservatives, libertarians and populists.

Frank G. Meyer, ed.	*What Is Conservatism?* New York: Holt, Reinehart & Winston, 1964. An anthology of essays by twelve leading conservatives.
George H. Nash	*The Conservative Intellectual Movement in America.* New York: Basic Books, 1979. A detailed description of the conservative intellectual movement in America from 1945 to 1975. It identifies the most prominent conservative thinkers and their works.
Peter Navarro	*The Policy Game: How Special Interests and Ideologues Are Stealing America.* New York: John Wiley & Sons, 1984. Clearly identifies the differences between liberals and conservatives in an issue by issue breakdown.
Kevin P. Phillips	*Post-Conservative America: People, Politics and Ideology in a Time of Crisis.* New York: Random House, 1982. A conservative theorist claims America is both post-liberal and post-conservative, and the forces shaping America's new philosophy are nonintellectual variables, such as population shifts and its fading economic fortunes.
Plato	*The Republic.* Benjamin Jowett, tr., New York: Modern Library, 1982. A classic and seminal treatise on political theory. Plato outlines what he believes should be the composition of the ideal political state.
James C. Roberts	*The Conservative Decade: Emerging Leaders of the 1980s.* Westport, CT: Arlington House Publishers, 1980. Profiles of 100 young conservative leaders.
Randall Rothenberg	*The Neoliberals.* New York: Simon & Schuster, 1984. A sympathetic yet critical analysis of the current status and prospects of neoliberalism, including a listing of its most prominent advocates and theorists.
William A. Rusher	*The Rise of the Right.* New York: William Morrow, 1984. An overview of the development of the conservative movement by one of its founding fathers and the current publisher of the *National Review.*
George H. Sabine	*A History of Political Theory.* 4th ed., New York: Holt, Rinehart & Winston, 1973. One of the most acclaimed texts outlining the

history of political thought from ancient times to the present. The book is an excellent introduction for any student seeking the roots of the contemporary political spectrum.

St. Thomas Aquinas

Political Ideas of St. Thomas Aquinas: A Selection from His Writings. New York: Free Press, 1973. A broad selection of the political writings of St. Thomas taken from various parts of his works. The readings emphasize his attempt to reconcile divine, natural, and human laws.

John S. Saloma III

Ominous Politics: The New Conservative Labyrinth. New York: Hill & Wang, 1984. A comprehensive study of the individuals and groups that make up the American Right by a liberal political scientist.

J. Salwyn Schapiro

Liberalism: Its Meaning and History. New York: Van Nostrand, 1958. Part one traces the basic ideas of liberalism as they have developed in principal Western democracies. Part two is an anthology of important liberal readings. Very concise, it reads like an outline.

Jay A. Singler

The Conservative Tradition in American Thought. New York: Capricorn Books, 1969. An anthology of the most significant work of individuals who shaped conservative thought in America. The introduction has a helpful overview of the origin and definition of conservatism.

Jay A. Singler

The Liberal Tradition in American Thought. New York: Capricorn Books, 1969. An anthology of American liberal statements, with an introduction that concisely explains the basis of liberalism in a historical, American perspective.

Peter Steinfels

The Neoconservatives: The Men Who Are Changing American Politics. New York: Simon & Schuster, 1979. The editor of a liberal magazine analyzes the neoconservtive movement and its founders.

James L. Sundquist

Dynamics of the Party Systems: Alignment and Realignment of Political Parties in the United States. Washington, DC: The Brookings Institute, 1981. Places current political trends in a historical and theoretical perspective and offers a unique view of the political spectrum.

Paul Tsongas	*The Road From Here: Liberalism and Realities in the 1980s.* New York: Alfred A. Knopf, 1981. Presents a case for a "new liberalism" in eight areas of American life, building on the past accomplishments and values of liberalism.
R. Emmett Tyrell	*The Liberal Crackup.* New York: Simon & Schuster, 1984. The conservative founder of *The American Spectator* chronicles the slippage of liberalism into a diseased "New Age Liberalism," citing chapter and verse of its current ills.
Herbert F. Vetter	*Speak Out Against the New Right.* Boston: Beacon Press, 1982. Twenty-two leading liberal thinkers from a variety of disciplines argue with the policies of the new right on a number of issues.
Peter Viereck	*Conservatism.* New York: Van Nostrand, 1956. Part one traces the historical and philosophical origins of conservatism. Part two presents principal conservative readings. Very concise, it reads like an outline.
Milton Viorst	*Liberalism: A Guide to Its Past, Present and Future in American Politics.* New York: Avon Books, 1963. An excellent overview of the liberal tradition in American politics by a nationally noted journalist. The book provides many interesting comparisons between conservatism and liberalism.
James G. Watt	*The Courage of a Conservative.* New York: Simon & Schuster, 1985. A former Reagan cabinet member presents a case for "modern conservatism."
Robert W. Whittaker, ed.	*The New Right Papers.* New York: St. Martins Press, 1982. An anthology of twelve prominent spokesmen for the "new right" addressing a variety of political issues.
Peter Witonski, ed.	*The Wisdom of Conservatism.* New Rochelle, NY: Arlington House, 1971. A four-volume anthology of important conservative writings.

Index

ABOUT THE EDITORS

DAVID L. BENDER, a history graduate from the University of Minnesota, has an MA in government from St. Mary's University in San Antonio, Texas. He taught social problems at the high school level for several years. The founder of Greenhaven Press, he is publisher of the *Opposing Viewpoints Series* and has edited many of the titles in the series.

BRUNO LEONE received his BA (Phi Kappa Phi) from Arizona State University and his MA in history from the University of Minnesota. A Woodrow Wilson Fellow (1967) and former instructor at Minneapolis Community College, he has taught history, anthropology, and political science. In 1974-75, he was awarded a Fellowship by the National Endowment for the Humanities to research the intellectual origins of American Democracy. He has edited numerous titles in the *Opposing Viewpoints Series*.